The Journey and Promise
of African American Preaching

. . . affords both clergy and laity a scholarly and wholesome look over the ways in which our forebears have come on the journey of faith and hope. He bids us to lift every voice and proclaim with wisdom, prophetic confrontation, and priestly listening—his 'trivocal' method of preaching—a way in which it can resound in the pulpit, the parish, and the podium."

—*Evans E. Crawford Jr., Dean Emeritus, Andrew Rankin Memorial Chapel, Howard University; Professor of Social Ethics and Preaching, retired, Howard University School of Divinity*

"Kenyatta Gilbert has made an invaluable contribution to homiletic scholarship and literature. Rich in tradition and wisdom, *The Promise and the Journey of African American Preaching* captures the genius of the African American pulpit. This work will be read widely and with great appreciation for years to come."

—*Richard Lischer, Duke Divinity School;* author of The Preacher King: Martin Luther King Jr. and the Word That Moved America

"Kenyatta Gilbert offers here a scholarly, personal, thought-provoking, and practical guide to the best practices in black preaching. The working preacher will find this model both a challenge and resource for promoting balance between the prophet, priest, and sage."
—*Leslie D. Callahan, Senior Pastor, Saint Paul Baptist Church, Philadelphia*

"This book immerses readers in a sophisticated, multivoiced soundtrack. Kenyatta Gilbert persuasively calls for ministers to preach in three voices—prophet, priest, and sage. He also amplifies keynotes from other disciplines such as practical theology, cultural studies, and pedagogy. As the Bible says, 'Faith comes by hearing.' After hearing this book, your faith in preaching will be renewed."

—*Brad R. Braxton, Distinguished Visiting Scholar, McCormick Theological Seminary*

"This analytical and critical tool for preaching in the twenty-first century is excellent for classroom, private study, and (Dr. Gilbert's debt for this brilliant teaching ii will help a new generation to gain and retair creative powers and prophetic drumbeat of t

Olivet Institut

The Journey and Promise
of African American Preaching

KENYATTA R. GILBERT

Fortress Press
Minneapolis

THE JOURNEY AND PROMISE OF AFRICAN AMERICAN PREACHING

Copyright © 2011 Fortress Press, an imprint of Augsburg Fortress. All rights reserved. Except for brief quotations in critical articles or reviews, no part of this book may be reproduced in any manner without prior written permission from the publisher. Visit http://www.augsburgfortress.org/copyrights/contact.asp or write to Permissions, Augsburg Fortress, Box 1209, Minneapolis, MN 55440.

Scripture quotations are from the New Revised Standard Version Bible, copyright © 1989 by the Division of Christian Education of the National Council of the Churches of Christ in the U.S.A. Used by permission. All rights reserved.

Cover image: Detail from *Aspects of Negro Life: From Slavery through Reconstruction*, Aaron Douglas. Used by permission of Schomburg Center / Art Resource, NY
Cover design: Nicole Summers
Book design: PerfecType, Nashville, TN

Library of Congress Cataloging-in-Publication Data
Gilbert, Kenyatta R.
  The journey and promise of African American preaching / Kenyatta R. Gilbert.
     p. cm.
  Includes bibliographical references (p.   ) and index.
  ISBN 978-0-8006-9627-6 (alk. paper)
  1. African American preaching. I. Title.
  BV4221.G55 2011
  251.0089'96073—dc22   2010053838

The paper used in this publication meets the minimum requirements of American National Standard for Information Sciences—Permanence of Paper for Printed Library Materials, ANSI Z329.48-1984.

Manufactured in the U.S.A.

15 14 13 12 11 1 2 3 4 5 6 7 8 9 10

For my beloved Allison
and our threefold cord
Olivia Copeland, Ella Jane, and Ava Sage

Contents

Acknowledgments

This work has been a journey in self-discovery. Its production symbolizes far more than the culmination of years of study and ministry experience. These printed pages reflect my profound indebtedness to a great cloud of witnesses who have provided unerring counsel and effectual prayer throughout this uneven yet gratifying journey. There is one person above all others who deserves my deepest gratitude for her continual support of my efforts and understanding during the research and writing of this book: my best friend and wife, Dr. Allison Blow Gilbert. Our three daughters, Olivia, Ella, and Ava, are to be acknowledged as well, for their lives began during the difficult season of doctoral studies and early stages of teaching. Their tender affections for me and gift of real presence are without comparison. My parents, Mrs. Elwayne and the late Reverend Robert L. Gilbert, and my nonagenarian maternal grandmother, Luetta Jefferson, who I affectionately call "Madear," tutored me in perseverance and taught me the value of learning. It is my sincere hope that this work honors their sacrifices on my behalf in some meaningful way.

I wish to express my special thanks to my teachers from grade school to graduate school. I am greatly indebted to my "Doktormutter," Dr. Sally A. Brown, a brilliant mentor and friend, whose encouraging words, thoughtful criticism, time, and attention to my work helped me to realize that such a book could be written. I am deeply grateful to Drs. Peter J. Paris and James F. Kay for seeing me to my dissertation's finish line. I would also wish to acknowledge Dr. Cleophus J. LaRue for first stimulating my scholarly interest in the African American preaching traditions.

I also express my thanks to Louisville Institute and Howard University for providing me time, space, and ample resources to devote my energy to writing this book. To those Texas, New Jersey, New York, East Africa, and Maryland/DC congregations whom I have had the privilege to serve in ministry, I thank God for you. To my dean, faculty colleagues—especially Drs. Evans Crawford and Gene Rice, Howard's "living sages"—and my students at Howard University School of Divinity, I am grateful for your assistance and encouragement. To Louisville Institute, whose funding provided me a short season to write, and to my guild, the American Academy of Homiletics and the Society of Biblical Literature, thank you for allowing me to road test many of the ideas in this work in a critical community.

Finally, I extend my heartfelt appreciation to those dear family members, friends, and colleagues whose love and support was indispensible to the completion of this work: my siblings, JaJa R. Gilbert, "a keeper of hope," and Evangeline R. Slaughter, "my doting Big Sis"; Samuel J. Gilbert Sr. ("Uncle Jack") and family; LaRue Gilbert Dorsey "Aunt Boo"; the Jefferson, Jackson, and Gilmore families; my spiritual mentor, Mr. Adrian Backus; my lovingly supportive in-laws James and Marietta Blow; Luke A. Powery, "my brother from another mother" and faithful conversation partner on the homiletical road; Lawrence Hibbert, "my unfailing encourager and prayer partner"; Lenon Phillips; Byron and Millicent Wess; Mark and Heather Johnson; Pearlie Beverly, Deborah Hoy Jones, Guy and Sherry Mollock, Paula Hall, Michele V. Hagans, James Logan, Keynon Akers, Karen Miller, Ajit Prasadam, Ray Owens, Rob Hoch, Audrey Thompson, Angela Lewis, Briggie Stansberry, Dante Quick, Toby Sanders, Gregory Ellison II, Wayne Croft Sr., Patrick Clayborne, Jonathan Walton, Brian Blount, Dale Andrews, Debra Mumford, Dr. Alyce McKenzie, Richard Lischer, David Lott, and, finally, I am grateful to my superb graduate research assistants Bridgette Nevils and Terra Dodson. Indeed, my cup overfloweth!

Introduction

A threefold cord is not easily broken.

—Ecclesiastes 4:12b

I have listened to sermons all of my life. My paternal grandfather, the late Reverend Benjamin Franklin Gilbert, was a tenth-grade-educated preacher who served as pastor to two small country churches, alternating weeks between the two of them. Family legend has it that among the rural Black reverends in the central Texas region he was deemed the "Dean of the Country Preachers." His unofficial homiletics course met around his home porch. My aunt LaRue, who eavesdropped on these sessions, tells me that he always had useful advice for the newly licensed ministers who would come sit and listen. That advice, she said, was usually a word or two about what homileticians today describe as the sermon's focus and function, central idea, or relevant claim. According to my aunt, he would say to them, "If you are going to talk about a dog in the sermon, then talk about a dog, not a cat. But if you are going to talk about the cat, then don't talk about the dog, talk about the cat." He continued, "There is enough to say about a cat to make one good sermon." According to Grandpa Benny, sermons that deviate from their topic inevitably fall flat. With that advice there was also a caution: "If you decide that it is the dog instead of the cat that you are going to talk about, remember, no one sermon can say all there is to say about the dog. Sermons that say more than they should are overwhelming to the listener's patience."

Beyond tips on sermon method and taking caution to remain sensitive to the listener, there remained a more significant counsel, some of which was passed on to my father. Taking a page from Grandpa Benny's folk wisdom, my father, also a working preacher, would say to the ministers-in-training that served our church: "Seventy-five percent of your sermon is the life you live."

My father, now deceased, took up the clerical duties to those two rural congregations after his dad's death. Though in many ways apprenticed by his father, my dad's ministry would ultimately take its own unique path, for, unlike Grandpa Benny, he had the benefit of a formal education. Though not seminary trained, in 1967 my father earned the distinction of being Baylor University's first African American graduate. After his graduation and upon concluding his services to those rural churches, he accepted a call to become pastor of the Carver Park Missionary Baptist Church in Waco, Texas, shortly after my birth. An author, community organizer, elected school-board official, and director of Upward Bound, an educational program preparing youth for college, during his tenure at Carver Park my father became a leading voice from Waco's African American community.

My father was deeply committed to the work of ministry. His commitments were less than modest. Despite the fact that for all of my life he was a severe arthritic who either got around on crutches or was carted about in a wheelchair by my brother JaJa or me, in his fifty years of life, through pain and joy, provision and lack, support and abandonment, he remained devoted to the biblical call to "preach in season and out of season." For him, preaching was a sacred assignment and the primary vehicle for humanity's spiritual and social liberation. As I reflect back on his dedication to the preaching ministry, I now realize what was at work in him and in his preaching. There were three dimensions to his preaching life. At times the voice of prophet raged in him; other times, in spite of and because of his afflictions, the priestly voice of compassion emerged; and still at other moments, the voice of sage spoke wisdom to those ministers who shadowed him. He was a minister of the gospel who preached *trivocally*—that is, his preaching ministry had the substance of the gospel in three-dimensional scope.

For most attendees, Sunday worship at Carver Park represented the end of a morally testing and spiritually hazardous week, a time to meet God at the well once again. Often enduring great physical pain, each Sunday, after taking a sip of water, my father would greet his awaiting congregation with the words, "Let the church say, 'Amen.'" He would offer a prayer of illumination, then open his Bible and begin reading the Scripture for the day. Following this, he would twice announce the subject of the sermon, the second time for effect, and gracefully move into exposition of the text. The sermon set-up was just as important as its close. Proceeding on, with embodied speech awakened to the Spirit's prompting, he would preach with all of his might. Three-quarters of the way through, in a low pitch, he would begin a rhythmic chanting. On most occasions this ritual would evoke "talk back" from the congregation. Nearing the sermon's close, he somehow found syncopation with the vibrating chords of the Hammond organ chiming underneath his voice. Putting measured speech to rhythmic verse, the chanting swelled into a full-throated cadence. By this point, he started moving the hearer into a captivating retelling of Jesus' Passion—his suffering death on Calvary's cross, his glorious resurrection and ascension and promised return. Dad excelled in the cathartic art of calling forth the *Amens* already present on the people's hearts, to use the words of Evans Crawford.

Having been firmly rooted in the singing-preacher tradition of many Texas preachers of his day, before offering his personal testimony he would round out his sermon with one of the time-honored songs in his repertoire such as "His Eye Is on the Sparrow" or "I've Learned How to Live Holy." As familiar as his testimonials were to me, they were not perfunctory. They were a thoughtful recapping of some life-altering event he had experienced or major obstacle he or another church member had overcome. Their purpose was to give the gospel "feet" into the listener's human situation. My dad's testimonials always spoke of God's love and power; they were confessions about miracles; they were his offering to the people to encourage their continued trust in the goodness of the Lord. Finally, the invitation to Christian discipleship, referred to as "opening the doors of the church," would be offered. For the repentant ones now welcomed home this was their opportunity to experience God's grace and a community's renewed support. To the unbeliever escorted down the aisle toward the altar, this was their opportunity to publicly receive the key of salvation.

This was the weekly ritual. Dad took it seriously. His preaching life was my orientation to the ministry of spoken Word and practiced Word. And, yes, my remembrances probably paint too romantic a picture. But the truth is, despite his many imperfections, errors in judgment, and the forgiveness he required from his family and community for his ministry-at-all-costs mind-set, he was truly a remarkable man. His life's grammar told a story about the preaching life as ministry of the Word, and the remarkable poetry of the gospel he consistently proclaimed and sought to demonstrate was that, in preaching, the hope of God speaks, and the words spoken are always words about divine intentionality, what God desires and what God expects. Robert Lewis Gilbert bequeathed to me a hunger to participate in the recovery of the African American preacher's voice in our times. It is my job to offer ideas about how to do that.

Recovering the Preacher's Voice

I believe in the providence of God. I was a political science major with a minor in religion at Baylor. Early on in my matriculation, following my father's death, I discerned a call to preach, but it took some "running and pleading" before I finally relented. I finished college with the intent to apply to law school, having spent two internships with my local congressman in his local office and one summer in Washington, D.C. However, divine interruptions did not support my intent. Instead, my acceptance of God's call to preach translated into a call to seminary preparation. I enrolled in Princeton Theological Seminary, during which I served congregations in Machakos, East Africa, and in Brooklyn, New York. Following my graduation and a brief tenure as an associate pastor in Brooklyn, I returned to Princeton, where some years later, I earned my PhD.

My father was this larger-than-life personality in Waco. After his death I struggled to find my way emotionally, intellectually, and spiritually. I felt burdened by it all. But these pivotal moments are what led me to accepting God's call. Curiously, although I had obtained tremendous knowledge and wisdom from observing my father's ministry, it was my mother's quiet nudging that gave me license to discover my own path. Still today, consistent with her and my father's admonishments in my early childhood, I hear her voice saying to me, "You ought to answer when you are called." I have heard this echo, in evolving translations, throughout my ministry-life preparations. My dad's death gave me wings; my mother's blessing supported my flight.

Some have said to me, "I see that you are following in your grandfather's and father's footsteps." Honestly, I never know whether such a remark should be taken as a compliment, condolence, or condemnation. Whatever is intended, I have learned over the years that every minister called by God is uniquely assigned to a specific work to be carried out in specific contexts during a specific season of time. The legacy traits that

I own are manifestly that—traits. As I now journey on in life as both a teacher and practitioner of preaching I recognize that the needed clarity about one's ministry purpose happens in the journeying process itself. My homiletics course meetings are not gatherings around Grandpa Benny's front porch, nor are my ministry engagements the Sunday-to-Sunday ritual from my father's wheelchair pulpit. I would like to think that my preparations have afforded me a movable pulpit—a much more versatile and reflective space to teach, preach, shepherd, and shape the minds of a new generation of ministers. If our calling means anything to us we should answer when God calls. But not only this; if we are to discover our authentic preaching voice we must answer the call with our own tongue.

I now teach homiletics at a historically Black, university-based theological institution in the nation's capital. Each semester I give a tone-setting talk to students who file into my introductory preaching course. Though some come with modest concern for preaching, most of them come with "how-to" expectations, on the hunt for tips to cram into their homiletical toolboxes. Then there are those who have come to piece together or integrate knowledge obtained from their biblical studies and theology courses. Still others are present with hopes of conquering their fright of public speaking and simply to complete the course with a good grade to show for their efforts. Honestly, I never know who will strive on with me or drop the course.

For good or bad, accompanying the student is always the "stuff" of their lives—personal baggage, narrow theological views, and long-cherished assumptions about what makes for good preaching. At the outset, I know that I will have my work cut out for me and that I must quickly come to grips with the task at hand. Our time together is limited, always too short. Thus, my aims for the course are straightforward. I want my students to recognize what makes for sound and faithful preaching; to discover what their lives uniquely offer to the preaching moment; and to find or recover their authentic preaching voice. Each semester I seek a creative encounter with God in the teaching and learning environment, and I want my students to realize the manifold possibilities of finding new channels for hearing and sharing the gospel in our times.

After matters of housekeeping (checking attendance, introductions, review of the course syllabus), I give them their first assignment. I ask each student to write down the names of their top five preachers. I assume, perhaps presumptuously, that every person enrolled has at least one name to put forward. But there is always reticence when this question is posed. Their quizzical stares communicate that I have made a deeply personal request—that I have asked them to put it all on the table, then and there, without the benefit of them first getting to know me. I make this request to plant a necessary seed toward helping each of them find his or her voice. Whether we are or are not conscious of it, whoever we regularly listen to, it is that person's voice that enters the pulpit with us, and that other's voice may at first be one we need, acting as guarantor of sorts or a necessary comfort. But more often than not that companioning human voice, which covertly is broadcast through our vocal channel, undermines our own voice—the voice that must speak in its own tongue. I repeat to them, "I want to know your top five preachers." They must take the leap. I task them with taking a risk to name those whom they esteem. No preaching takes place without risks involved.

As providence would have it, I am not permitted to interlope without having to answer the question, "Professor, who are your top five preachers?" The temptation to call the roll of the pulpit masters is hard to resist. Martin Luther King Jr., Gardner Taylor, Prathia Hall, Samuel Proctor, Harry Wright, Caesar Clark, my father, and a number of other saints are those whose homiletical imprint I bear. But my response to them is rather simple: "The preachers I deem exemplary are those who have discovered along the way their authentic preaching voice." There is something mysteriously powerful about the authentic clarion call. Somewhere along the way, preachers such as King, Hall, and Proctor found their preaching voices, and as a consequence have found enduring veneration in the culture, whether they have preached the gospel in the small local church or on the national or international stage.

I am convinced that the preacher begins to learn to preach when his or her words are exhausted and at the moment when his or her ears become open to the revelation of God. The first class ends with this confession: "I can't teach any of you how to preach. That's not my task. I am here to help you to find your own voice among the multiplicity of others that vie for your allegiance." African American preachers today must find their voice in this presently inhabited world. That is, they must begin to think more radically about ways to address contemporary concerns by joining God in the radical work of dismantling the social order's program of *disvocalization*—the muting of the preacher's voice. The most important responsibility of African American preachers today is to find again in their own speech a speaking God and to recognize that their voice as preacher is vitally determined only through the person and work of Jesus Christ and the indwelling of the Holy Spirit. For only a voice determined in this way, as late pastor and revivalist Manuel Lee Scott so aptly puts it, proves useful for the community's realization of hope in a society bent on unvoicing the preacher.[1]

Jesus' Vision and a Vision for Preaching

African American preaching today is more threatened than one ever could have imagined, as are the churches and communities in which it is practiced (as I will explain in the next chapter). It must now overcome its own apparent irrelevance in an increasingly pluralistic, postmodern age of intense spiritual, social, and economic crisis. But make no mistake, preaching is the single most important task for staving off the death of African American churches and communities today. As Samuel Proctor writes, "No one in society has as much responsibility as the preacher for altering our perception of the world around us from that of a chemical-physical accident to the handiwork of a loving, caring God."[2]

The most fundamental task of the preacher is to interpret Scripture within human community, in service to Jesus Christ. As principal interpreter, the preacher who assists the worshiping community to negotiate faithful ways in moving toward the goal of the actualization and maintenance of the God-human relationship, as pastoral theologian Jacob Firet describes it, acts as that community's resident practical theologian.[3] This fundamental task shapes the preacher's functional identity and understanding of self. Never standing above the Word, the preacher who goes to Scripture as a sacred duty on the congregation's behalf is one entrusted by God and community to understand, nurture, and nourish the church's life in critical and constructive ways. The preacher's role as interpreter of the Word is critically important. But also important is the hearing community's function to become lead appraisers of the preacher's message and not merely passive receptors. Three factors are particularly challenging: (1) too many African American preachers only entertain rather than truly preach; (2) congregations are more passive, expecting to be entertained rather than challenged and encouraged to reenact the gospel in their daily lives in ways that are fresh and make sense for the current generation; and (3) some of the technological advances we are so fond of in our culture encourage passivity: television, Internet, cell phones, social networking sites, and the like. The challenge is to use that technology but make it liturgically useful and practical, more personalized, relational to encourage and empower others to restore and make a difference in their communities.

What is there in African American preaching today that keeps it from sliding into nothingness? Inviolably, Jesus' inaugural vision described in Luke 4:16-21 is the basis for the preacher's discourse and what makes preaching essential for the restoration of African American villages.[4] The preacher is licensed and ordained to walk lock-step with this vision; otherwise hearers wither on the vine. But how should the African American preacher's understanding of the preaching ministry be defined? What should be derived from Scripture to inform the preacher's understanding of self? Are the preachers who have captured the sacred imagination of the contemporary Black religious public faithful adherents to Jesus' norm-setting vision for Christian proclamation, where in Luke 4 the principal requirements are clearly outlined?

> When he came to Nazareth, where he had been brought up, he went to the synagogue on the sabbath day, as was his custom. He stood up to read, and the scroll of the prophet Isaiah was given to him. He unrolled the scroll and found the place where it was written:
>
>> "The Spirit of the Lord is upon me, because he has anointed me to bring good news to the poor. He has sent me to proclaim release to the captives and recovery of sight to the blind, to let the oppressed go free, to proclaim the year of the Lord's favor."
>
> And he rolled up the scroll, gave it back to the attendant, and sat down. The eyes of all in the synagogue were fixed on him. Then he began to say to them, "Today this scripture has been fulfilled in your hearing."

Often this passage is narrowly interpreted. Its sociopolitical character is explicit. But this passage beckons us to see more. Jesus is not only announcing himself here but, in his reading the scroll, he also is rallying the community to reclaim their religious obligations to serve God by expressing concern for the community's well-being. A communal-care agenda first set in Isaiah 61 is to be acknowledged by the cultural gatekeepers of tradition.

This points out for them that this fact—community wellness—is a divine concern. Their hope for a messiah reiterates the fact that life in Galilee is less than perfect. The oracle calls into question social arrangements that exploit the poor and religious rituals that baptize the status quo. But also captured in this self-referential prophecy is Jesus extending an invitation to discipleship. To declare his mission to the world is to invite a response to the God of Scripture. Jesus proclaims fulfillment of Isaiah's prophecy with the declaration, "Today the scripture has been fulfilled," but a brief glance at our postmodern world in relation to the text's original auditors makes apparent the fact that the work to be accomplished is far from completion. Jesus declares to this Galilean community that he is the one they have been anticipating. Put another way, the embodiment of God's concern for a society that is broken has finally arrived.

Not all of the Galilean citizenry were hopeful and expectant. Why would hope be an option for the blind and the poor in this setting when the communal predicament for the marginalized undoubtedly has been generationally enduring? Naturally those present in the synagogue that day were keepers of hope for a coming messiah to appear at some time in history, but it is not plausible that those on the margins of society had anything for which to be hopeful. The astonishing revelation for me as I consider what the text seems to say is that the messianic promise finds fulfillment indeed, but those who react to the reading are ostensibly not the ones who would most obviously benefit from its message. Nonetheless, Jesus' recitation makes an obvious claim on the entire community, for those present and absent, because implied in what Jesus gives witness to and is anointed to perform is grounded in grace and mercy that is offered to all. An entire community receives an opportunity to experience new life at God's expense, but this opportunity I believe is unbeknownst to some segment of that society. Messianic hope becomes incarnational reality for this community. Spiritual and physical salvation has come in the person of Christ. An alternative to social decay is proposed and those who gather at this public forum are first to receive the news. The spirit and message of the gospel captured in Jesus' words, "He has sent me to proclaim release to the captives . . . recovery of sight to the blind, to let the oppressed go free," are instructive for any preacher who would dare to preach in the Jesus tradition.

New Testament scholar Brian Blount suggests that the "meaning potential" of a text such as this one should not be restricted to the classical canons of textual and ideational biblical interpretation alone where "meaning is understood to reside within the formal boundaries of a particular text's language."[5] Rather, what should be explored and examined is the meaning potential of texts in relation to the interpreter's interpersonal interactions with texts—namely, attending to the contextual elements in the society wherein such texts are situated. Interpreters always come to texts with their questions, preunderstandings, and concerns. Thus, since no interpretation of a text is prejudice-free, according to Blount, interpreters are themselves a part of the interpretative results. Therefore, to give one's exclusive focus to textual and ideational concerns of this Lukan text in disregard of the interpersonal is to miss the Scripture's offer of another revelatory channel. One major implication, then, is that an interpreter's failure to consider the interpersonal dimension is to leave oppressed voices, like those to whom the text refers, on the margins and out of the interpretative process.[6] What does this mean for Black preachers? It means that the spoken Word from Black pulpits must demonstrate how a text functions and has meaning in the lived experiences of Black people.

This Scripture lesson in Luke's Gospel continues to matter, to speak, and it speaks a vision not yet fully realized as it still invites our participation. Therefore, if the African American village's state of health is to be recovered in our times, then out of the vocal waterway of the African American preacher must come Jesus' vision and message. Only then can African American preaching reclaim its proper identity, its catalytic function of nurturing and nourishing the prophetic, priestly, and sagely dimensions of the preaching ministry, and be profitable for our times. Though blurred today, Jesus' vision summons our participation in the radical work of bringing good news to the disinherited ones; lighting the way for those who sit in darkness, guiding their shadowy existence, and liberating the multitudes whose dignity-robbing wounds of spiritual and physical despair require more than band-aid dressing. Knotted up in Jesus' life-world and message, as recorded in Luke 4:16-21, is the self-portrait of the gospel in threefold scope.

African American Preaching as Trivocal Preaching

African American preaching[7] is more than an artistic expression; it is foremost an act of worship. It is ministry of spoken and embodied Word in service to the gospel of Jesus Christ for the community. In other words, it is proclamation of good news that *does* something—it names, provokes, encourages, teaches, and inspires faith—on God's behalf. Indeed, African American preaching uses the power of language and art to interpret the gospel in the context of Black misery and Christian hope. What is intriguing about African American preaching as an act of worship and ministry practice is that it is truly catalytic, holistic, and most completely actualized only when marked by three constitutive orientations—the scriptural voices of *prophet*, *priest*, and *sage*, which, theologically, follow a trinitarian pattern. Together, when these voices function in a mutually influential relationship and are synthesized and appropriated in one's preaching life, they become what I describe as *trivocal preaching*.

When I use the term "African American preaching," I am referring primarily to this three-dimensional dynamic at work within the tradition and brought into its proper focus (although, in many veiled or unfocused ways, a particular dimension or voice is often privileged over or used in disregard of the other). Thus, my working definition of African American preaching—or what I call trivocal preaching—is:

> African American preaching is a ministry of Christian proclamation—a theo-rhetorical discourse about God's good will toward community with regard to divine intentionality, communal care, and the active practice of hope—that finds resources internal to Black life in the North American context.

Given the broad range of complex congregational and secular community concerns and expectations, only the voice of the African American preacher, which reclaims for Black preaching its catalytic function of nurturing and nourishing the prophetic, priestly, and sagely (wisdom) dimensions of the preaching ministry, can hope to be profitable in a violent, fragmented, postmodern, and increasingly pluralistic world. My argument is very simple: *African American preaching, at all times, absconds its character and charge to the church and the public unless it recovers its elemental prophetic, priestly, and sagely voice.* Through this threefold cord the preacher finds her or his voice—a voice that speaks words of justice, recovery, and hope, telling again the church about its present situation and where it must now go.

Before proceeding, it may be helpful to clarify the nature of the three voices of trivocal preaching that are used repeatedly in this book. I use the scriptural images of prophet, priest, and sage to distinguish the dimensions of the threefold voices sought in contemporary preaching practices in African American churches and communities, noting that each image shares a common structure for homiletical interpretation.

The Prophetic Voice

The prophetic voice is a mediating voice of God's activity to transform church and society in a present-future sense based on the principle of justice. The prophetic voice speaks of divine intentionality—what God demands and expects of God's own human creation. The basic biblical feature of this discourse is that it opposes idolatry, particularly self-serving and self-deceiving ideologies. It refuses the temptation to absolutize the present; it drives toward a new, unsettling, unsettled future. It is a word that speaks to the predicament of human suffering from the perspective of God's justice. This speech, at all times, assumes a critical posture over and against established power. Last, the prophetic Word is a word of relentless hope.[8] Still, beyond this formal theological place, the prophetic voice of the African American preacher has traditionally had a certain disposition toward rhetoric and poetic imagination that is brought to bear in the American context in which Blacks find themselves.

There is a creative element here. First, there is a pedagogical dimension of the prophetic voice of Black preaching that accents the importance of enabling the congregation to understand its situation in light of God's justice and what God intends. Second, there is an aesthetic dimension that reveals the tremendous creativity and deeply rooted rhetorical imagination and expression of Black preaching. The tragedy to be overcome by way of this voice is the African American preacher and church's disregard of the past and scriptural tradition and also the endless insecurities that paralyze faithful action in the present. Though beginning in slavery, Black churches virtually institutionalized the prophetic principle in many distinctive ways—recognizing injustice far and wide—yet it does appear that the prophetic principle has been cloaked or abandoned in many African American church contexts today.

The Priestly Voice

The priestly voice is a sacramental mediating voice of Christian spiritual formation that encourages listeners to enhance themselves morally and ethically by integrating elements of personal piety, that is, keeping to devotional practices like daily prayer and Bible study, and striving after holiness through abstention from cardinal sins. Bequeathed from the Revival period (see chapter 2), the priestly voice of most Black Christian pastors, in rural and urban settings, places greater emphasis on moralistic concerns. It has given primacy to the individual's spiritual well-being and God's evaluation of the believer's life upon Christ's return over temporal, social justice–centered concerns.

The priestly voice of Black preaching emphasizes the importance of congregational worship and being justified, redeemed, and sanctified by Jesus Christ's atoning works. Furthermore, it focuses on the preservation of the cultic apparatus—the gathering place for worship—making church administration, financial stewardship, and church attendance safeguards of the institutional life of the church. Most important, the priestly voice calls the gathered community to prayer, which means that the role of preacher carries with it the functional obligation for the work of intercessory prayer within and for the community at large. In other words, faithful execution of preaching as priest is to recognize that there are no substitutes for the "ministry of presence."

Like the prophetic voice, the priestly voice interprets and mediates the requirements of covenantal obligation to God and to God's people, reminding them of God's faithfulness and promise keeping. Slave preachers often acted as mediators or priests between the slaves and the slaveholders, speaking and petitioning God on the community's behalf concerning the actual conditions of slave life; but, for risk of life, they seldom challenged the oppressive slave system publicly. While the biblical prophets are portrayed as oracles who spoke as God's mouthpiece, the priest's message more explicitly carried a stronger interpretative function of God's activity in the world. The second principal part of the priestly voice is its stress on matters of congregational care, specifically in the aftermath of natural disaster or oppressive life situations. Often through priestly Black preaching the preacher guides individuals into a religious encounter or experience with God. Thus, the preacher's active presence and human speech becomes a psychic, physical, and spiritual healing resource. Despite this, many would claim that the priestly voice is primarily the voice of religious and communal socialization, which focuses almost entirely on parishioner needs while having little impact on the wider society.

The Sagely Voice

The sagely voice is a conferring and peculiarly communal voice of biblical wisdom and realistic hope for future generations that daringly speaks within the context of radical social and ecclesial change for the purpose of keeping vital the congregation's vision and mission. The sagely voice is a wisdom-focused, dialectical, communal voice of both preacher and hearer. Sages interpret the common life of a particular community of worshipers. The sagely voice carries an eldering function; it strongly corresponds with the voice and activity of the African *jaili*. In West African lore, the *jaili* (poet) used praise singing and storytelling and functioned as the repository of the community's oral tradition. Of the three voices, the sagely voice is the most overlooked, primarily due to Black religious practices that are preoccupied with the ethos of contemporary culture, which ascribes greater worth to present-future preaching interests.

The sagely voice interprets the congregation's historical and cultural legacy, namely, its archival materials, and seeks to decode the complex signs, symbols, and texts of a congregation's worship life. Through the sagely voice, ideally, the preacher preaches God's Word in authentic partnership with the community. For example, in some African American churches, on special occasions such as a church anniversary, there is a tacit assumption that the preacher knows the history of the church and will faithfully interpret it and inspire those to honor it in their continued witness of their own participation in the historic journeying as a congregation trusting in God. Or, in some denominations the high participation of preaching by lay leaders gives some description about the nature and function of the sagely voice.

Ostensibly, with such a communally shared witness in many African American congregations, one could consider, at least conceptually, that the sagely voice is most clearly evident in the call-and-response ritual. As Evans Crawford rightly expresses it, the [sagely] preacher has to have "a good ear, a homiletical ear to work with folk idioms, an ear attuned to the people."[9] That is why, in this paradigm, "the true 'resident theologian' is deemed to be the congregation itself . . . [and this] affirms the corporate nature of the preaching event, and highlights the significant role the congregation can and should play in the shaping of theology for proclamation."[10] Nowhere has this voice been so materially expressed than in the social justice movements of the 1950s and '60s, when, under Martin

Luther King Jr.'s clarion call, African Americans boycotted and marched in pursuit of human dignity. It is the sagely voice that is little consulted by younger Black preachers in the postmodern era; as a result, the signs of a community's sacred historical and cultural legacy are increasingly disappearing.

If African American preaching is to overcome its apparent irrelevance in today's society, preachers must find again their voice in Jesus' vision for Christian proclamation. The preacher who goes to Scripture on the community's behalf must be the lead investigator in the search to understand the complex needs of people of African descent in this country in particular, and the human community across the globe in general. African American preaching can only be relevant and useful in an increasingly pluralistic and fragmented world when it is an expression of God's good and perfect will for wellness in African American churches and community. More than passionate and persuasive speech, at its core, preaching of this kind is Spirit-guided, three-dimensional, anointed discourse that speaks of divine intentionality, communal care, and the active practice of hope.

African American Preaching as Practical Theology

The need for contemporary African American preachers to reconceive vigorously the prophetic, priestly, and sagely[11] voices of the preaching ministry is vitally important, because these voices, in religious practice, have become indiscernible or isolated from one another. These voices of Christian faith practice are complementary in both nature and function. I will even make the bold claim that to ascribe any static or fixed label like "prophetic preacher" to the Christian preacher is biblically and theologically shortsighted. No preacher is always prophetic if he or she proclaims the Word in the Jesus tradition and is faithful to preaching the whole counsel of Scripture. Furthermore, some Black preachers are sufficiently radical but insufficiently self-critical. Under the guise of being prophetic, preachers who take delight in detailing the mortal and venial sins of their listeners or, for that matter, bringing criticisms to oppressive world systems that dehumanize persons on a regular basis "without tears in their [own] eyes" are preachers who have lost sight of the grace of God in their own life.[12] Preachers of this sort abuse and wound the people of God.

A holistic view of African American preaching does not rest easy with carving out distinctions that ignore the interrelatedness and interplay of the prophetic, priestly, and sagely voices. For preaching to matter today within African American churches and communities demands that preachers refocus their ways of representing themselves as ministers, so that they might more clearly signal an understanding about the complex needs, circumstances, and aspirations of a particular community. The particular and dynamic matrix of self-understanding I am proposing in this book involves African American preachers becoming more self-aware about why today they must more explicitly convey in their sermons, and in their actions that stem from them, a preaching life that is earnest and authentically Christian. Only when African American preaching reclaims its catalytic function of nurturing and nourishing the prophetic, priestly, and sagely dimensions of the preaching ministry as a Christian practice is it instructive in and profitable for our times.

My perspective for this work is twofold. Doing theology from the sacred desk is unavoidably particular, and an apt description of the precise nature and function of African American preaching is only obtainable when its historic journey, aesthetic genius, and trajectory are thrown into the light of critical interdisciplinary reflection. This involves a careful analysis of the biblical, theological, historical, and sociocultural elements appearing in African American preaching. One way to delve deeply into the reservoir of African American preaching's seemingly unconnected dance of Scripture, culture, body, and voice is to enter the conversation from the vantage of practical theological reflection. I define practical theology as the theological, empirically oriented, interdisciplinary field that reflects on the critical and constructive theory and concrete praxis relationship dynamics that relate to Christian religious practice.

Few contemporary proposals in homiletics are intentionally interdisciplinary. Interdisciplinary reflection is not unique to practical theology but in recent years it has increasingly become a gold standard in many of the theological disciplines. As it has once been claimed, "All roads lead to Rome," a similar age-old adage rings true: "All theological roads lead to preaching." While much of my cross-disciplinary reflections are undergirded by sociological and historical perspectives on African American churches and communities, theology is taken seriously in this work. To interpret homiletically through the lens of practical theology is to think in terms of interconnections, relationships, and systems, giving attention to the interactive dynamics of the spoken Word, circumstances, and contexts from which and to which words are spoken.[13] My creative aim is to reclaim a more robust homiletical theology for African American preachers, which reflects, in many ways, my own understandings, faith commitments, and normative views of the Christian faith. In other words, I do not write as a disinterested interpreter.

This book is methodologically significant because I bring together a reflective framework that deliberately follows the logic of the four tasks consensus model of practical theology, outlined in Richard Osmer's recent work *Practical Theology: An Introduction* (2008). I organize this book around the four core tasks (descriptive-empirical, interpretive, norms of practice, and pragmatic) of practical theological interpretation that give us a helpful framework for addressing the following questions. The descriptive-empirical task asks the question, "What is going on in African American preaching today?" The interpretive question asked is, "Why is African American preaching more threatened than ever imagined?" The norms-of-practice task asks, "What ought to be going on in African American preaching today?" And finally, derived from a careful consideration of the previous "how-to" informed by the "why-to" questions: "How might African American preaching be shaped to embody more fully the normative purposes of the Christian faith?" These four tasks often interpenetrate one another and relate to one another in spiraling or circular fashion, which means they invariably circle back to a task that may have previously been explored.[14]

Chapters 1 and 2 describe why trivocal preaching is the single most important task for staving off the death of African American communities today and trace the historical origins of African American preaching in North America. Chapter 3 demonstrates how the use of the scriptural images of prophet, priest, and sage and the basic tenets of three models of interdisciplinary work in practical theology reveal a great deal about our theological understanding of African American preaching. Chapter 4 offers a practical plan for developing the sermon as a form of theological reflection. Also, to illustrate how trivocal preaching might come to expression as a form of holistic Christian proclamation through the mutually enriching prophetic, priestly, and sagely voices, I lend my own sermonic voice to the conversation. In chapter 5 I show how the trivocal dynamic works in sermons preached by Martin Luther King Jr., Prathia Hall, and Gardner Taylor, and round out the conversation by illustrating how other contemporary preachers draw on these voices in the ministry of preaching. Finally, in chapter 6 I have designed a typology of seven personas or functional roles taken on by contemporary African American preachers, to help readers think more deeply about the intricate lifeworld of the Black preacher. Here I call African American preachers and their congregations to a deeper awareness of and commitment to *trivocal preaching* in the multiple contexts of African American life, naming, in concrete terms, what is at stake for the village if "we preach not the gospel" in our times.

As you read this book, I hope you will begin to understand better the vital role preaching plays in the health recovery of African American churches and communities, and that as a result of your encounter with these thoughts you, too, will participate in significant ways in the transformation of congregations and communities in African America and beyond its increasingly permeable walls.

The State of African American Preaching Today

Follow the grain in your own wood.

—HOWARD THURMAN[1]

The spoken Word in America's Black pulpits has long been esteemed for its persistent calls for justice, church reform, moral and ethical responsibility, and spiritual redemption. These commitments have been central to the Black church's identity. More importantly, though, these commitments to the spoken Word provide a way to take up the more fundamental matter of how one may, for example, determine what relational continuities exist between the prophets, priests, and sages of Scripture and the basic character of the Black preacher's peculiar speech and communal obligations.

I set out working on this project with three primary audiences in mind—the student of homiletics,[2] the working preacher, and the teacher of preachers. These are the individuals I know best since I am a former seminarian, an ordained minister, and a teacher of preachers. But not only this, I have come to view this book as generating a productive friction of sorts among Black homiletical theorists. Though my work, in some respects, builds on earlier scholarship, this book takes the tack that claims that critical reflection on African American preaching is, on the one hand, relatively underdeveloped and, on the other, vying for more forward-thinking scholarly discussion.

A critical analysis of the state of twenty-first-century African American preaching can unfold in a number of ways depending on how one thinks the picture should be painted. It is important to begin our conversation about the state of African American preaching today from three frames of reference: (1) theological education and the intellectual tradition of contemporary African American homiletics; (2) the broad range of congregational and secular community concerns and expectations; and (3) the character and moral agency of the Black preacher. By focusing in this way, we are provided a wider lens to investigate what is at stake in contemporary preaching practices in African American churches and communities.

Learning Habitats and the Preacher's Humanity

Contemporary homiletics has insufficiently attended to theological matters pertaining to incarnation and the historical conditioning of culture, and how these matters shape the message of the gospel in different contexts. A number of African American homiletical theorists echo this claim, having now sufficiently demonstrated in their scholarship that African Americans are subjects of their own histories rather than objects under someone else's principles of scrutiny.[3] Despite this, across the lines of race, ethnicity, and culture, homiletical proposals have in general uncritically accepted many Enlightenment presuppositions, tending toward foundationalist assumptions for preaching, specifically, the commitment to embracing claims to knowledge in some fundamental certitude. One-size-fits-all homiletical methods do not work because our thinking about preaching is ever evolving, always subject to challenge, and definitive interpretations are thus difficult to find.

Our current picture of theological education, namely the way clergy leaders are trained to preach, is an outflow of circumscribed ideals that follow theoretical principles and guidelines, techniques and approaches that are supposedly historically and culturally neutral.[4] Predictably, for both student and homiletics instructor, the classroom setting often does not become transformed space for authentic Christian praxis. Having attended a predominantly white seminary where Eurocentric theological points of view are privileged I quickly learned that doing well in preaching class carried with it the expectation that I would cope with and conform to a particular set of homiletical norms without questioning the authority of them.

Participants bring their own conceptualizations, convictions, mores, and folkways—those emanating from local congregational life—to the classroom setting. The sensible homiletics instructor will take great care to help each student stave off the ensnaring trap of cultural abandonment and feelings of disconnection from their actual preaching habitats and context-determined ways to preach. Learning to preach involves one's conscious resistance to forces that strive to domesticate one's voice. That is why the role of the pedagogue is so important. Theological seminaries and divinity schools often become principal players in the domestication process. When I have taught courses in predominantly white settings the chief complaint of students of color is one that centers on the issue of cultural invasion. Cultural invasion is the act of the teacher—who becomes invader—imposing his or her own worldview upon students in ways that inhibit their creativity by dismissing, camouflaging, or curbing their expression.[5]

One inattentive to the vital role context plays in African American preaching, for example, will hardly notice the indigenous character of the "chanted sermon," and may not perceive it as theo-rhetorical artistry and experienced Word. Despite the common portrayal of the Black folk preacher as comic figure, James Weldon Johnson has rightly expressed: "The old-time Negro preacher . . . was an important figure and at bottom a vital factor. It was through him that the people of diverse languages and customs who were brought here from diverse parts of Africa and thrown into slavery were given their first sense of unity and solidarity."[6]

In recent years, even some African Americans have come to disdain this preaching style. I believe this is in part due to its misuse in the hands of charismatic charlatans. One might also point out the fact that preachers from many "high-brow," "silk-stocking," "demure" congregations consider some communities "low class" or "uncouth." This may be less true in some historically Black denominations—Baptist, Church of God in Christ (COGIC), and African Methodist Episcopal (AME)—and more true in the so-called mainline denominations, for example, Episcopal and Lutheran. But more than that, contemporary homiletics, it seems, continues to privilege African American preaching modes that seem to cohere best to the nomenclature of white academicians. To be precise, when the African American "chanted sermon" is attempted or examined in academic contexts without regard to the actual preaching habitats from which the "chanted sermon" arises, not only will context-determined ways of listening be overlooked, but also missed is the aesthetic genius of this preaching style's interconnected dance of Scripture, culture, body, and voice. Like the Negro spiritual, there is a subtext, an internal logic, to the authentic "chanted sermon" that is only accessible when the hearer is helped by cultural history.

This known fact should inspire creative pedagogy as well as encourage greater sensitivity to what is fitting for hearers. "One of the tasks of theological education," writes homiletician Richard Ward, "is to help more of the student's story become available for reflection as a [learning] resource."[7] This means, of course, that teaching methods must be constantly scrutinized to guard against self-serving acts of cultural invasion that consciously or unconsciously devalue the contributions of pupils who have much to share from their own socio-ecclesial habitats. Because cultural identity and religious formation are principal determiners of how a sermon will be preached and heard, one truly committed to the work of transforming churches and communities through the gospel of Jesus Christ will "pay attention" to the vital importance context plays in preaching. Our preaching contexts matter when our concern is the gospel. For this reason, to understand the Christian faith contextually "is really a theological imperative."[8] There is no gospel "for us" that is not clothed in human culture and is not mediated through the sociocultural concerns of where we live, who we are, and what we value. Constructive pedagogy asks if our theologies of preaching are constructed with the local idioms of our students in view. In an age of suspicion hermeneutics, competing narratives, and reality redescription, without a revised understanding of what is at stake culturally and communally in contemporary preaching, our homiletical theorizing will be scantily useful.

Black Homiletics Coming of Age: Two Leading Proposals

Since the release of Henry H. Mitchell's *Black Preaching* in 1970, considerable attention has been devoted to carving out Black preaching's nomenclature in academic reflection, and rightly so. But only a few proposals since then have furthered the discussion of Black preaching beyond contrasting it with Eurocentric preaching, most notably that of homiletician Dale Andrews.[9] Given this impasse, the future direction of African American preaching remains indistinct. In order to provide some context for thinking about the intellectual tradition of African American homiletics, and to reiterate the importance of attending to matters of context in Christian preaching, I now draw our attention to the homiletic scholarship of Henry H. Mitchell and Cleophus J. LaRue.

Henry H. Mitchell: Event and Experience

The consistent refrain in Henry Mitchell's landmark work *Black Preaching* and subsequent magnum opus *Celebration and Preaching* (1990), which emerged twenty years later, is that context matters and must never be overlooked if our concern is preaching. In 1970 Mitchell's intended readership had been mostly African American, but in his more recent reflections he anticipates both an African American and Anglo American readership. On the heels of the great civil rights social revolution, Mitchell's scholarship soared as it invited a multiethnic readership into a primarily oral religious tradition. In *Celebration and Preaching,* Mitchell states that preaching's goal is to reclaim "heart religion," that is, to counter the objective and detached preaching approaches that only appeal to the cognitive aspects of one's being. With this orientation, he works to synthesize elements of the "mainstream" Protestant pulpit tradition and Black church pulpit traditions. Identifying the rhetorical dynamics in both streams, the preacher finds right entry into what he labels "experiential encounter." He argues that the coalescence of rhetorical vehicles—guidelines of concrete images, familiar language, familiar details, timing of impact, and so forth—when understood and appropriated by the called preacher, promotes encounter and hence can reach people at the core of their belief.

For Mitchell, the authentication of Black preaching has all to do with human reception of the spoken Word. In the sermon event the congregation rouses the preacher to a celebratory high point characterized by chanting, humming, or moaning under the auspices of the Holy Spirit. This momentum-building sermon event forms the distinctive worship ethos where Black preaching is made visible. In other words, without congregational response, there can be no genuine Black sermon. By this paradigm, the sermon, as Mitchell defines it, is "reasonable and relevant sequences of biblical affirmation planted in or offered to the intuitive consciousness of hearers, by way of what might be called homiletical coworkers with the Spirit."[10]

In Mitchell's theory of celebration, the intuitive consciousness and emotive consciousness are the locus points for faith formation. In the spoken Word, they are the listener's pathway, sectors of one's belief system and worldview.[11] Intuitive consciousness or emotive consciousness is faith forming. It honors, reflectively, one's gathered life stories; it is the seat of one's tastes as well as prejudices. Relative to faith insights gathered from intuitive consciousness is always this stream that defies rational examination. Because the intuitive realm is built upon gathered stories— "tapes," if you will—the preacher's principal concern is helping listeners "to improve these 'tapes' or habitual replays of response to particular circumstances."[12] Still, the emotive consciousness grounds the celebratory dimension of his theory.

This biblically based, unanalytical phenomenon of celebration, as Mitchell claims, is an expression of joy in God. According to Mitchell, celebration has five central commitments: (1) it frees up the listener to experience the spontaneous workings of the Holy Spirit in worship; (2) it fosters a deep connection between the hearer and the sermon's subject matter; (3) its contagion is infectious in the context of worshipers in fellowship; (4) it honors the fact that emotion is essential to the ecstatic enforcement of the Word for the people; and (5) it promotes identification when rhetorical details and imagery are placed before the hearer during the sermon.[13] Mitchell's clear rejection of the old homiletic preaching models, first developed by early-eighteenth-century neoclassical rhetoricians, which equate the sermon with rational argumentation through propositional speech or logic, is clear. In fact, his emphasis on experiential encounter links him to the stylistic, performative tradition of the sixteenth-century elocutionists and, more evidently, to theorists of the New Homiletic.[14]

The New Homiletic movement began in the late 1960s and gained momentum following the proposals of several homiletical theorists, most notably Fred Craddock, Eugene Lowry, and Charles Rice. According to the New Homiletic school, effective preaching of the gospel is dialogical, imaginative, primarily narrative in form and inductive in movement, and shaped to the listener. These theorists prize preaching that unfolds inductively instead of through propositional logic. Hermeneutically, there are three major implications in relation to preaching from this perspective:

(1) the Word of God must be spoken; (2) preachers must see themselves as listeners; and (3) the fundamental nature of the spoken Word is a community-creating event. Put differently, the theological and hermeneutic trajectory of the New Homiletic perspective is that preaching is an *event and experience* concerned with "message bearing" and interpreting the Word of God freshly in the way of reality in the vernacular of the people.[15] Though theorists in this movement such as Mitchell view preaching as "creating experience," it is not always clear what is actually being said about God that creates the experience.

Clear of the vestiges of old-school homiletics, Mitchell's working hermeneutic seeks distinction in Black preaching through the matrix of language. In his view, Black preaching conforms to certain patterns of language indigenous to Black culture.[16] Despite his good insights concerning the relationship of African culture and its influences on Christianity in Black churches, one of the most contestable claims he makes is that Black preaching "requires the use of 'Black language'—the rich rendition of English spoken in the ghetto."[17] Few would consider this a hallmark since there is no consensus about what constitutes "Black language." It is more accurate to say that Black preaching is always responsive to and mindful of the vernacular of the people. Clearly, rhetorical interests drive Mitchell's preaching theory; so the "message-bearing" task of the preacher is what reveals the essence of Black preaching.

Cleophus J. LaRue: Belief and Marginalization

Insofar as the term "Black preaching" describes a rich tradition of varying theological orientations and methods of sermon construction and delivery, Cleophus J. LaRue finds Mitchell's theory lacking. Hence, LaRue provides a counterclaim. He argues that as important as oral formulas, emotion, and vivid images are, the problem with highlighting traits of Black preaching as foundational properties of what makes it distinctive is that this "is merely describing characteristics of a process already in motion."[18] LaRue privileges an interpretive framework to identify what makes Black preaching distinctive. Whereas Mitchell's programmatic goal is essentially performative-rhetorical, LaRue's goal involves a formative biblical-hermeneutic plan to demonstrate the role and function of Scripture in sermons preached by Black clerics. The distinctiveness of Black preaching, maintains LaRue, lies in the way African Americans conceive of God and hermeneutically appropriate Scripture to their lived experience. He maintains that there are three central dynamics at the heart of Black preaching: (1) belief in an all-powerful, sovereign God; (2) a Black sociocultural context of marginalization and oppression; and (3) the Black lived experience.[19] Black preaching, expresses LaRue, is formed, reflected upon, and organized through what he terms "domains of experience." LaRue claims there are five domains that (1) provide a descriptive vehicle for categorizing broad areas of Black lived experiences, and (2) create a resource bank for ideas for the content of the Black sermon.[20]

The first domain is *personal piety*. Sermons emanating from this domain strongly cohere to the tenets of American evangelicalism (e.g., keeping devotion, practicing personal discipline, and good moral conduct). Sermons birthed in the *care of the soul* domain tend to focus on pastoral care matters—the health and wellness of individuals, encouragement to the bereaved families, and so forth—and are usually prescriptive in nature. The *social justice* domain is the realm where matters pertaining to local and national public policy, issues of race, classism, and gender equity are of central concern. Sermons originating in the *corporate concerns* domain raise concern about more specific crisis issues of the community such as violence in inner cities, wealth and educational disparity among Blacks and whites, Black incarceration and recidivism, and the HIV/AIDS epidemic. Finally, the *maintenance of the institutional church* domain is characterized by an emphasis on the ecclesiastical or cultic life of congregations. Sermons growing out of this domain have principal concern with matters such as church growth and building projects, financial stewardship, religious education, and missions. "When the preacher speaks of life out of one of these domains," asserts LaRue, "a bonding takes place between preacher and congregation because the listener senses that the preacher understands some meaningful aspect of his or her life."[21] Both preacher and sermon play critical roles within the communal experience of African American Christians.

Will It Preach, Still?

Scholarship written with sensitivity to the significant role that contextuality plays in Christian practices is of paramount importance. Satisfying descriptive proposals reflecting on African American Christian practices in the United States today are generally hard to find. This is true, specifically when one considers the thin slate of academic texts used in seminary settings that reflect on historically marginalized communities. Theological educators usually separate these works out from the core; they are typically viewed as supplemental in nature. According to African American theologian Stephen Ray, this phenomenon by and large comes as a response to the fact that much of the work of African American theologians originates in critique of some normative male-Eurocentric theological view. Ray notices that the privileges and pitfalls of such texts as *Celebration and Experience* and *The Heart of Black Preaching* have to do with their highly contextualized nature. On the one hand, these texts imply that white normative voices may be seen as in need of correction, while still their own normativity is not called into question. On the other, what is communicated is that the genius of Black scholarship and focus on historically marginalized communities is found in criticism. This second consequence of these messages is perhaps the most unsettling; that is, that "this message is an agnosticism about the capacity of these originating communities to produce works that are generally constructive to the Christian tradition."[22]

Importantly, both LaRue and Mitchell have established nomenclature to discuss African American preaching in terms of Black religious and social identity in light of gross oversights in Euro-American pre-postmodern homiletic proposals on contextual matters.[23] These African American theorists perceptively demonstrate that preaching which matters never forms in isolation from culture. They both note the particular influence of African culture and American evangelicalism on African American rhetorical traditions. But in highlighting the significance of the Black sociocultural context for preaching, neither discusses, in any sufficient depth, what Black preaching must now do to overcome its apparent irrelevance in today's society. They place strong emphasis on positive stories worthy of celebration and views of what the Black experience is for Black people. But in their aim to describe the precise nature of African American preaching, mainly in ways exclusively tied to perceived harmonious question sets and experiences growing out of oppressive circumstances, both theorists, like their non-African American counterparts, hold too tightly to relatively fixed interpretations of "Blackness" and what constitutes a "Black sermon."

Is it the case that a sermon may be disqualified as "Black" if an African American preacher preaches cross-culturally or in a faith community where he or she is a racial/ethnic minority? Without much effort African American preachers tend to be carriers of culture wherever they preach. The most effective preachers happen to be those who keenly discern how to make certain adjustments in sermonic presentations based on the relational configuration of the preaching context. "Effective [preaching] is a transaction between [preacher] and [congregation] who comes to trust the [preacher] and thereby accepts the preacher's message" because it reflects authenticity to one's cultural self but also a sensitivity to the ways listeners from one context to another hear and process sermons.[24] Howard Thurman, Katie Cannon, Peter Gomes, James Forbes, Barry Black, Violet Fisher, and Brad Braxton are a few examples of Black ministers who have preached in historically Black religious settings, but also have clearly breached the standing "Black sermon" criteria highlighted above. The vocational commitments of these ministers have time and again summoned them to leadership roles in predominantly white, interracial, and multiracial settings. Postmodernity has ushered in new and tremendous challenges to any definitive claims to knowledge. Postmodern suspicion stains virtually every pew of every church of every religious community today.

In fairness, more recently LaRue has taken care to nuance some of his essentialist claims. In a recent essay he notes that the postmodern social and ecclesial shifting of African American culture is currently under way. He acknowledges that traditional Black worshipers whose operating hermeneutic centers on a God who acts mightily against an oppressed people may in fact not apply to all who now populate the pews on Sundays in African American church contexts. Several upwardly mobile Black listeners, claims LaRue, might indeed challenge the notion that their life experiences are or have been in any way akin to those who are oppressed on the margins of American society.[25] This is true, but it is also true that one is also called to look beyond one's own personal experience and look to larger communal concerns. Even the privileged should not live in a silo. As I am writing this, I, too, am well aware that some of my descriptive claims may be offset by future theorists who have inherited a different sociocultural homiletic landscape from my own.

Not only is an updated or revised description of "Blackness" needed to enrich our understanding of Black preaching in the twenty-first century, other proposals must now emerge in Black homiletics that, for example, focus on the character and moral agency of the Black preacher. If Aristotle is right when he maintains that the character or "ethos" of the speaker is highly significant to a speech's persuasive appeal, then the ethical character and moral agency of African American preachers are subjects that need more theoretical attention in Black homiletic theory. While no preacher's life is without stain or blemish, personal integrity and ministerial ethics ought to matter.

It is deeply vexing to know that even some of the most respected clergy in African America regularly preach on matters of ethical or moral conduct, while not holding themselves or expecting their congregations to hold them to the same standard. What is more perplexing is that congregations will overlook the most egregious behavior in an effort to protect and defend what is perceived to be the community's last "authentic" hero. The private life of preachers was less scrutinized publicly in the pre-Internet era. However, in today's sound-bite, texting, voyeuristic, and highly litigious culture, little remains private. Sadly, these known facts will be of no consequence to some segments of the African American church. There will be church communities that will continue to tolerate the unscrupulous behavior of their ministers as long as the preacher is furnished with charisma and yearned-for preaching gifts.

One final inquiry is warranted. If strong biblical content, the sociocultural experience, emotive appeal, and the awaiting congregation are requisite elements to the genuine Black sermon, then should not a clearer picture appear about what qualifies as prophetic preaching in the context of Black life in America? To date, few scholars have attempted to bring into focus the precise nature and function of prophetic Black preaching. Although, due to racism, the prophetic principle has been virtually institutionalized in Black churches since the independent Black church movement of the early nineteenth century, a satisfying description of the nature and function of prophetic preaching has ostensibly been unattainable.

Naming God and how God acts in the world is and has always been at the core of Black preaching; however, I would argue that still today higher esteem is given to *how* things are said (style) over *what* is actually being said (content). If this were not the case, there would be no point to my investigation. Preachers must rally the people around a vision of God that motivates those persons to act decisively in the process of transforming lives and systems in African American villages. A village made whole first requires that the preacher's character find congruence with her or his speaking. The messenger and the message spoken to the people must be scrutinized and held up in the light of God's good news in Jesus Christ.

Apostle Paul's announcement, "I punish my body and enslave it, so that after proclaiming to others I myself should not be disqualified" (1 Cor. 9:27) should be both a caution and a homiletical lesson for the preacher.

Naming the Crises in the Village

Martin Luther King Jr. once preached that the answer to the blighting of hope is to confront one's shattered dreams and to ask oneself, "How may I transform this liability into an asset, transform this dungeon of shame into a haven of redemptive suffering?"[26] King's rejoinder was simply this: adhere to infinite hope. Adherence to infinite hope, proclaimed King, is not the bitter acceptance of fatalism nor is it palliative hope that renders individuals passive and incapable to speak out for change. Rather, adherence to infinite hope is to cling to realistic hope. Adherence to realistic hope, suggested King, is the only viable upshot to a community's death. Obviously hope becomes unavailable if the community's preachers are unwilling first to name the crises of our times as finite disappointment. For only then is adherence to infinite hope possible or, more contemporarily speaking, the audacity to hope possible.

Robert Michael Franklin's recent book *Crisis in the Village* focuses on the multiple crisis points within African American "villages," specifically, the local neighborhoods and communities with predominantly Black populations in the United States. He lists a range of urgent issues to be confronted and puts forward a series of strategies for healing the "village." Healing the village, says Franklin, entails determining and setting priorities and finding viable solutions that correspond with positive enduring values, community assets, and resources within African American communities. Thus, the place to begin the social transformation and needed restoration of hope is with the "anchor" or "mediating" institutions of the village—the Black family, Black churches, and Black schools.[27]

Franklin claims that Black congregations have become confused about the mission of Jesus Christ. The gospel of love, service, and justice, Franklin rightly states, has become supplanted by "personal greed, obsessive materialism, and unchecked narcissism."[28] Moreover, Black congregations are far too uncritical about America's routine way of permitting and rewarding inequalities of wealth and power, and this, too, contributes to the prosperity gospel's encroachment within Black religious life. This problem is aggravated by the shameful silence of Black clergy on major policy issues, those having specific implications for the Black community in particular, says Franklin. The community's job is to make clerics accountable for their actions and inaction. One way to do that is to make them craft and proclaim their vision for the community's social and religious transformation.[29]

The complex of problems that militate against the health of African American villages—high incarceration rates, father absenteeism, unwed and teenage pregnancy, domestic abuse and violence, high rates of sexually transmitted diseases, high foreclosure rates, homelessness, joblessness, job discrimination, unaffordable health care, unscrupulous pay-day lending practices targeting the Black working poor—is an albatross strangling the lifeblood out of America's African American communities. I am arguing that *trivocal* preaching has the capacity to stem the tide of death of the village and supply hope to persons who desperately need spiritual care and social justice when it adheres to and announces Jesus' norm-setting declaration in Luke's Gospel. The preacher's words matter when they speak justice and hope into being, when preachers act as servants to their communities, interceding on its behalf and mediating God's moral, spiritual, and ethical concern for Christian unity. When the preacher takes the position as sage, that is, the community's trusted guide and repository of the community's wisdom, future generations rise to make great contributions to the cause of Christ. In the next chapter I explore the historical journey and rise of the Black preacher in American society and the long legacy of trivocal preaching.

2

A Venerable Yet
Vanishing Tradition

*He [the Priest or Medicine-man] early appeared on
the plantation who found his function as the healer of the sick,
the interpreter of the Unknown, the comforter of the sorrowing,
the supernatural avenger of wrong, and the one who rudely but
picturesquely expressed the longing, disappointment, and resentment
of a stolen and oppressed people.*

—W. E. B. Du Bois[1]

*The black preacher, especially in the South, is king in a private kingdom.
Whether learned or ignorant, he is both oracle and soothsayer, showman
and pontiff, father image to all and husband-by-proxy to the unattached
women in the church and others whose mates are either inadequate or
missing. More than a priest, he is less only than God.*

—James Farmer[2]

The Rise of the Black Preacher

The obvious place to begin an exploration of the historical origins
of African American preaching is the African continent.[3] Recognizing first the particular influences African culture and American slavery
has had on African American cultural communication is critical. The

classic Herskovits/Frazier debate in African American studies importantly addressed the question of African retentionism in Black communities in the United States. In *The Myth of the Negro Past*, Melville Herskovits argued that there was evidence of African cultural forms among Blacks that persisted through slavery. These cultural forms served to differentiate aspects of African American culture from the culture of their Euro-American counterparts. E. Franklin Frazier disagreed with Herskovits's thesis. Frazier believed there were few, if any, remnants of African culture in the United States. From his perspective, in the aftermath of slavery's distressing effects the fabric of the African American family was destroyed. In the way that the family system defined the core of African societies, Frazier believed that Africans in America had to organize a new culture around the church and other social institutions.

Notwithstanding the merits of Herskovitzs and Frazier's views, later scholarship reveals inadequacies in both perspectives. To a great extent, culture is transferred from one generation to the next. "The primal, clan-oriented, monotheistic, if operationally polytheistic religions of Africa," according to Gayraud Wilmore, did indeed find deep resonance with the religious sensibility of the African in slavery. Blacks did not use Christianity as whites first introduced it to them without making certain substantive changes that took into consideration their oppressive condition and other contextual factors. The religion of the slaves brought to America, from the beginning, was a *tertium quid,* a collision of worlds, "something less and something more than what is generally regarded as Christianity."[4] In other words, Black culture is transferred from one generation to another and is continuously transforming, taking on new forms, which means the substance of cultural meaning seldom dies. This observation is critical if we are to bring into focus the historical significance of African American preaching in American society.

African Orality

In various parts of Africa, the poet is called a *muntu*, which among other designations means "prophet." Words spoken by the *muntu* transforms things into "forces of meaning, symbols, and images."[5] The *muntu*'s evocative and creative expression of African rhetoric is defined as *nommo*—the sacred power of the spoken word to create and generate reality.[6] This creative character of the word calls the world into being. Through the

African poet, it is believed that God speaks and what is spoken establishes the cosmic order. Everything comes into being through the voice, and, according to Molefi Kete Asante, "the contemporary African preacher in the African American church is probably the best example of the power of *nommo*."[7] But an important distinction should be noted: whereas the Christian preacher stands under the Word and to proclaim its witness, *nommo* declares that humans have mastery over the word, which is to say that from the very beginning the word is with the *muntu*.[8]

Numerous cultural signatures—rhythmic cadence, intoning, whooping, measured speech, use of metaphor, word picture, playfulness, gravity—that many contemporary Black preachers apply with homiletical imagination emanate from the influence of early slave preachers, and perhaps more so from their precursors, the medicine man and conjurers. Lamenting the broken history of the earliest records, historian Eugene Genovose supposes that slave preachers may have had a wider range of religio-spiritual functions in slave society than commonly thought:

> Every plantation had its exhorter. The great pity is that so little is known about his relationship to the black preachers who passed through and so little about the relationship between both the black preacher and the plantation conjurers. It would not be surprising if some black preachers were all three at once.[9]

Slave preachers had specific roles and responsibilities to the community. They acted (1) as seers interpreting visions and the significance of events; (2) as pastors calling for unity and communal solidarity; and (3) as messianic figures provoking the first stirrings of resentment against oppressors.[10] Since the emergence of slave societies, Africans in America have retained various identity forms, aesthetically and poetically, that have influenced communicative social and religious practices.

Preaching in Chains

Whether manifested in singing, dancing, and speaking in tongues in rural, urban, or suburban African American congregations or storefronts, descendents of the African slave have carved out a liberating space for creative expression in Christian worship practices. Wilmore observes that the Africans' seeming lack of concern for doctrinal fidelity to the accepted standards of Christianity during slavery was not due to a void of theological and moral content in their own West African religious traditions and ontological systems. Rather, their perceived duality revealed a more practical concern. The experimental quality, practical elements, and profound symbols of the African's sacred cosmology—belief in a Supreme Being who presides over and orders the spirit world—required no explicit theological translation in the West.[11] In contrast to erected boundaries of the sacred by Europeans and Americans, in slave society the Africans' black bodies, not parchment, became sacred texts. In viewing the "body as sacred text," the revelation of God to the African took on a radically different meaning in contrast to the African's white counterparts.[12]

Israel's exodus saga, for example, functioned as a powerful motif for the communal story of Africans in the American slavery context in ways that it could not for white Americans. Emancipation was interpreted through the biblical story of the exodus. The Black church became a critical arena in the creation of prophetic and liturgical homiletical practices that embraced justice and freedom themes. "Through dramatic reenactments and ritual activity—preaching, singing, and praying—Black congregations collapsed the distance between the slaves of Egypt and the slaves of the United States."[13] The exodus motif is an essential part of Black Christianity's socioreligious imagination. Slaves intuitively recognized the inadequacy of the conventional "theology from above" that formed the basis for much of the Euro-American-influenced worship practices. Their encounter with God was different. God on the lips of those adhering to a "theology from above," paying scant, if any, attention to a God who comes as Incarnate Word, is a God far off. By contrast, encounter with God in much of African American worship practice is expressed along these lines, "our fathers/mothers cried and God heard their cries."[14]

It is the very disinheritance and dehumanization that inspired the African to hold in tension both a "theology from above" and a "theology from below." To comprehend the African's holy act of remaking himself or herself in the worship ritual is to perceive this liminal and tensive reality. The reconstructive elements of body, moral character, and belief in an Almighty God kept vital the converted Africans' faith and hope in Jesus, the disinherited One, who in life and death was triumphant over sin and evil. Faith in a God of justice inspired the African's prophetic criticism and holy rage. More important, through Christian symbols, Africans named their corporate struggle as sacred encounter with the Divine whom they believed would act decisively on their behalf.

We turn now to an investigation into the developmental phases of African American preaching in the United States and the advancement of the African American preacher. Each historical phase—Colonial North America, Revival Period, Reconstruction, Great Migration, Civil Rights, Post–Civil Rights—is crucial for tracing the origins of Black preaching, but in view of the most exponential changes in Black preaching occurring from slavery to Reconstruction (i.e., in such advancements relating to literacy, licensing, abolition, and the rise of independent churches), subsequent phases, which are in some ways less dramatic, will be given briefer attention in this chapter.

Colonial North America Period

The majority of slaves wanted to hear from their own Black preachers. Yet, seldom did these preachers challenge the status quo publicly. In spite of the slave preacher's displayed charisma, his words could really only mean accommodation to southern slave life. Both the reclusive life and the power to speak freely in open air became dammed up. "The preachers walked a tightrope . . . they had to rely on the protection of their masters . . . to preach the Word."[15] The old-time Negro preacher was primarily "responsible for the 'narcotic doctrine' for coping and survival epitomized in the Spiritual, 'You May Have All Dis World, But Give Me Jesus.'"[16] Consequently, the tradition of indirection, the skill to communicate with more than words, was essential to survival. Opposite any eye-dropper homiletical approach, "many [slave preachers] were able to preach effectively to all at once," marshaling, as a means of survival, "para-language—tones, gestures, and rhythm"—also known as call-and-response for those unable or unwilling to follow the written sermon.[17] Because almost all slaves were illiterate in the Colonial North American period, it is important to note the inescapable biases in the historical record, namely, that the history recorded about Black preaching was exclusively reported by white men, whose judgments about the Black preaching in slave society could only capture a shortsighted portrait of an indigenous tradition more expressly known by Black participants within the worshiping community. Youtha Hardman-Cromwell ably describes this historical infelicity when she writes:

Few sermons of nineteenth-century Black preachers, slave or free, are preserved in print. It is also true that because slave activities were closely watched, slaves became masters of deception and subterfuge. Their messages, like those passages of Scripture produced in times of persecution, were coded. It has been widely publicized how the spirituals were used as messages to effect the escape of slaves. Lesser known is the use of quilt patterns to send messages to help slaves escape. It is reasonable to think that the messages of the slave preachers were coded as well.[18]

One key development in the colonial period was the use of African spirituality in Black faith and Black preaching, a factor never completely lost during the long period of slavery. African spirituality greatly influenced the nineteenth-century courageous witness of unlettered, "unofficial" preachers and exhorters such as John Jasper of Richmond, Virginia. Jasper, the unmatched elocutionist whom one biographer called an "African genius," and others of the mold kept vital the folk religion of the "invisible church."[19] Slave preachers emerged as framers and innovators of an indigenous Christianity. In other words, their homiletical practices were particular and fitting to the social, psychological, and spiritual needs of Blacks. Cleo LaRue maintains that as early as the nineteenth century Black sermons exhibited a definite power and distinctiveness of their own. What contributes to the distinguishing character of Black preaching, argues LaRue, is the hermeneutical and dialogical interchange between the content of the Black sociocultural experience and the Black preacher's particular uses of Scripture and their awareness of God's presence.[20]

Another significant development born in the colonial North that had direct implications for subsequent eras was the issue of literacy in the slave community. Despite their own illiteracy in most cases, slave preachers, through personal magnetism and natural eloquence, had the capacity to organize and effectively lead religious communities. Thus, illiteracy did not hinder the spread of the gospel or the Black preacher's claim to ecclesiastical recognition. Black preachers were seen as outstanding leaders in the slave quarters.[21] They often acted as mediators between the slaves and the slaveholders. Subsequent to the failures of early missionary movements in the colonies such as the Church of England's Society for the Propagation of the Gospel to the Heathen in the Foreign Parts (1701), there was an increase of Blacks preaching to Blacks.[22]

However, the mission had two major drawbacks. First, the missionaries had underestimated the scope of the work to make converts. Because the missionary-to-slave ratio was greatly out of balance it was difficult to implement their agenda. Second, as a result of their dilemma, the duty of consistent pastoral care in the South was virtually impossible. Furthermore, and perhaps the Society's greatest obstacle, was its inability to counterbalance the racist mind-set of slave masters, who did not want baptism to alter the slave's civil position in society.[23] Nevertheless, not all of the SPG's missionary objectives went unfulfilled. For the purpose of catechesis, missionaries were able to capitalize on the conversion of slave-born children. Overcoming language barriers and understanding the geographic and work patterns of slaves were attributed to the mission's marginal success.[24]

Under white supervision, hardly any Black Christian preacher of the eighteenth century worshiping in the English colonies was licensed to preach. Black clergy were considered "jackleg," that is, unofficial preachers prior to the American Revolution in 1776.[25] According to Eugene Genovese, "most slaves heard well-trained and well-educated Black preachers once in a while."[26] Black plantation and itinerant preachers preached to Blacks and some whites. Those preachers who commanded respect of their masters were called "regular" preachers, and, ironically, were perhaps not proportionally more illiterate than their white preacher counterparts.[27] Still, the Black preacher's existence remained highly circumscribed. High levels of illiteracy, rejection of religious expression by whites, and the slaves' failure to truly develop a collective mission all contributed to a failing-to-thrive Black preaching ministry.

In his landmark text *Slave Religion*, Albert Raboteau reminds us of the slave's survival ethic, how outside the formal structures of the institutional church slaves constructed their own "invisible church" of prayer meetings and worship services, where the Black preacher wielded great influence. Up until the Civil War some Black preachers had large numbers of southern whites who heard their preaching. By the nineteenth century, however, Black preachers' progressive strides were severely curtailed in the aftermath of Gabriel Prosser's plot to rise against Richmond, Virginia, in 1800, Denmark Vesey's conspiracy in Charleston, South Carolina, in 1822, and Nat Turner's uprising in Southampton, Virginia, in 1831.[28] David Walker's denunciation of white slaveholders who operated as if Christianity and slavery were compatible best characterizes the mood of the times and Black insurrectionism's justification. Walker writes:

> I ask everyman who has a heart, and is blessed with the privilege of believing—Is not God a God of justice to *all* his creatures? Do you say he is? Then if he gives peace and tranquility to tyrants, and permits them to keep our fathers, our mothers, ourselves and our children in eternal ignorance and wretchedness, to support them and their families, would he be to us a God of *justice*? I ask, O ye *Christians!!!* who hold us and our children in the most abject ignorance and degradation, that ever a people were afflicted with since the world began—I say, if God gives you peace and tranquility, and suffers you thus to go on afflicting us . . . would he be to us a *God of justice?*[29]

Following Turner's bloody revolt, Black preachers of note either relocated to the North or fell silent.[30] Still, in the colonial North an opportunity was created for the slave preacher to rise to a platform that indirectly brought a level of respectability to the preacher from both Blacks and whites.

Given this reality, a final development must be acknowledged. The power and influence of Black preaching was enlarged in the period, not only for Blacks in slavery but in the minds of whites, whose fear of the Black preacher's message increased due to suspicions in the wake of potential slave rebellions and insurrections. Black preachers were tending to layers of concerns in this phase. In such abhorrent conditions, which brought direct assault on their humanity and survival, that they actually possessed an intense desire to preach the Christian gospel, a luxury for all practical purposes, demonstrated an indomitable character unique to Black preachers in this social world. They were able, in many ways, to transcend the abusiveness of their reality to focus on their spirituality. "The great accomplishment of the slave preacher was his ability to bend to the actual conditions of slave life and to transform themselves into teachers and moral guides with a responsibility to keep the people together with faith in themselves."[31] Despite the fact that Christianity made little headway in Black life during the first 120 years of slavery in North America, Black preaching gave the slave community its first visible role models and community leadership.[32]

Revival Period

Although the Black institutional church did not grow in colonial North America, Christianity itself grew through the invisible institution. Slaves converted to Christianity in large number during the religious revivals between the years of 1740 to 1822. The Revival period signaled a huge advancement in the formation of the Black preacher, especially in Baptist and Methodist denominations. An American, experiential, Bible-centered, and revivalistic brand of Christianity—evangelicalism—dominated the religious landscape by the early nineteenth century. Its egalitarian thrust was its most revolutionary trait as it created a turning away from the more contemplative Anglican worship rituals. Evangelicalism emphasized personal relationship with God in Christ, and belief in the direct action of the Holy Spirit to bring about emotional conversion for holy living. And so, as Albert Raboteau expresses, "Africans in America found great congruence with their lived experience and evangelicalism's fire."[33]

In contrast to Anglicans and Presbyterians, Baptists and Methodists provided the initial access and opportunity for Blacks to exhort and to preach without the overburden of a slow indoctrination process before baptism. At least initially, the revivals promoted a cultural shift in society that rebuffed any staunch commitment to maintaining economic and social class division. Representatives of all classes worshiped together at revival services. Consequently, Blacks and whites discovered a form of social acceptance not previously offered to them.[34] Stirring out of the 1801 Great Revival at Cane Ridge, socially the revivals accomplished three important things: they made Christianity more accessible; they created space for a freer, livelier style of preaching minus overtaxing educational demands; and they allowed the poor and enslaved to publicly preach and exhort.[35] But to understand the full range of impact of this period on the Black preacher and Black preaching, a brief description of the composition of the religious landscape is vital.

Donald G. Mathews claims that the early evangelical movement of the revivals transformed the culture socially and religiously. It elaborated on the emphasis that the Christian life required the confession of spiritual new birth and forming a personal relationship with God in the person of Jesus Christ through conversion experience. For whites, the revivals "offered direct contact with a God whom philosophers had cast in aloof obscurity." Differently, Blacks viewed the revivals as a way to reclaim some of the remnants of African culture in their foreign habitat.

> Moved to ecstatic trance by drumming, singing, and dancing Afri-
> can mediums spoke and acted in the person of one of their gods.
> Similarly, Afro-American evangelicals were seized by the Spirit and
> driven to act, speak, and move under its power . . . the slaves believed
> that they were filled by the Spirit of the Christian God and not pos-
> sessed by an African spirit.[36]

The implication, then, is that Blacks differed from whites in their ability to incorporate and adopt religious symbols in a new cultural sys-tem with relative ease. Mathews's conclusion is supported by the fact that "one of the most important links between African culture and black Christianity has been the absence of a sacred/secular dichotomy in tradi-tional thought."[37] Despite these obvious differences, liturgically, the reviv-als surfaced similarities. There existed an undeniable connection between evangelical services and behavior characteristics of spirit possession in African festivals. Revival participants mediated the divine message.

Together, but Unequal

Nathan Hatch identifies three reasons why Blacks, slave and free, swarmed into Methodist and Baptist churches during the Revival period: (1) they welcomed Blacks as full participants in their communities, at least ini-tially, and condemned the institution of slavery—however severe their retreat on the issue later;[38] (2) they proclaimed a Christianity that was fresh, capable of being readily understood and immediately experienced; and (3) most critically, in this period Blacks became Christians due to the emergence of Black preachers and exhorters. Consistent with Geno-vese's claim in the previous period, Hatch contends, Blacks wanted to be preached to by their own.[39] One cannot underestimate the pervasive distrust Blacks had for whites who professed Christian love and liberty on the one hand, while on the other justifying through Scripture Black subju-gation and social inferiority as God's will. Raboteau describes Anderson Edwards's working hermeneutic of suspicion that slave preachers had:

> When I starts preachin' the Gospel I couldn't read or write and had
> to preach what massa told me and he say tell them niggers iffen they

obeys the massa they goes to Heaven but I knowed there's something better for them, but daren't tell them 'cept only the sly. That I done lots. I tell 'em iffen they keeps prayin' the Lord will set 'em free.[40]

Donald Mathews argues that in spite of the early signs that white evangelicals were friendly toward freedom, labeling slaveholding as blasphemous and immoral, in the end their inability to find a solution to the problem revealed their general reluctance to fulfill the evangelical promise of "preaching liberty to the captives." Therefore, as a social, historical process, Mathews claims that in the appropriation of evangelical Christianity, southern Blacks, not southern whites, best embodied the spirit of the social movement that began in the late eighteenth century.[41]

The Spawning of Black Independent Churches

As to the circumstances surrounding ecclesiastical separation, the establishment of African American independent churches signified a major achievement in the period. A series of racial discrimination occurrences sparked former slave Richard Allen and other Black Methodists to begin conducting worship services separately from their white Methodist counterparts. The culminating event happened in November of 1792, when the African American members of St. George's Methodist Episcopal Church were barred from the first-floor benches they normally used in the worship service and proscribed to sitting in the church's gallery, which had been recently added to the church. St. George's African American parishioners obeyed the unfair command at first, until one of the white ushers told Black parishioner Absalom Jones, a respected man in his mid-forties, to move to the segregated section upstairs during the opening prayer one Sunday. Jones requested the usher wait until the prayer ended. But the white man insisted Jones move immediately. After Jones stood to his feet, and as soon as the prayer ended, Jones and the rest of the African American worshipers permanently departed from that church.[42] Following this, on April 9, 1816, Allen and a group of northern free Blacks from five congregations met at Bethel African Methodist Episcopal Church, organized by Allen and his followers, to discuss strategy for legal emancipation from their white Methodist parent body. A legal victory for Black Methodists in Pennsylvania's Supreme Court followed. Founder and organizer Allen became the denomination's first bishop.

Moreover, the independence achieved by the African Methodist Episcopal Church (AME) set off similar happenings among other Black Christians, namely, other Methodists and Baptists. Still, the proliferation of Black independent churches was not truly noticeable until the Reconstruction period. However, it is significant to note the time-honored heritage and moral vision of "racial uplift" that these early northern African Methodist ministers pioneered, which predisposed later clerics such as AME bishop Reverdy Ransom and AME Zion Reverend Florence Spearing Randolph to a more radical and holistic theological and social vision. Black Methodists were not split with whites over doctrinal issues or matters of polity. The inability of whites to respect Blacks as equals in Christian fellowship was in truth the fundamental grounds for separation. This notwithstanding, despite developing their own churches, Blacks still believed that some cooperation and expression of goodwill with white churches was indispensable to their survival. Regardless of the indignities Blacks suffered, "the most important reason for desiring a continuing association with the white churches lay in the moral and social implications of that ideal societal vision that has always inspired the black churches, namely, the vision of society in which race would have no significance."[43]

The Revival period brought about three developments in Black preaching: first, whites preached evangelism but not social equality either in the church or in the society at large. Blacks compromised their dignity—accommodating to racism—by becoming members of white congregations. Later, they had to split away to form their own churches in order to express their own dignity. That break was a prophetic move if ever there was one. In light of this paradoxical reality for Blacks in general and their leaders specifically, the most thoroughgoing development of this phase is summed up in Mathews's lucid claim, "The tragedy of southern Evangelicalism was not that institutions were unable to make white men behave as they should have, but that they could not allow black people full liberty in their Christian profession."[44] Despite the damaging effects of Southern Christianity, "black preachers were beginning to build their new Church with tools they had already crafted." Furthermore, contends Mathews, "the full model of southern Evangelicalism was the creation of blacks themselves; it was they who made southern religion different."[45]

Second, despite the profession of this southern brand of Christianity, what one finds significant is that through evangelicalism Blacks found some social advancement. To Blacks, the conversion experience phenomenon, unique to evangelicalism, continued to symbolize that all are one in Christ. And while the impulse of conversion for Blacks was not "revolutionary egalitarianism" during the revivals, it served the purpose of offering Blacks a means of establishing their claim upon the Christian care and respect of their comrades. A third development in this period is that Blacks understood the Christian message they had received from their own Black preachers. Their religious experiences were not defined and exemplified as organized doctrine on paper but what they did suggest was that Blacks had received the Christian message primarily as the primitive Christians had—as a message transmitted orally about God's act in history, which proclaimed "liberty to the captives."[46]

In the end, there were noteworthy advancements in the formation of the Black preacher during the Revival period, primarily through Baptist and Methodist denominations. But the message preached by Blacks was primarily repressive in that it was not liberating socially. The strong embrace of evangelicalism did translate into premillennialist quietism politically and religiously, which is basically a turning away from social activism to a passive expectation of an ideal society to be brought into being upon Christ's second coming.[47] Still, the decline of Anglican influence and the analogies between African worship style and evangelical revivals in the Revival period all point to the reality that Black preachers, slave and free, were able to make Christianity their own.

Reconstruction Period

Despite the development of Black preachers and the significant social and religious advancements of Blacks in the Revival period, the Reconstruction period, also called the Black Nadir, represented a time when freedom for Blacks proved incomplete. Immediately following the Civil War, set roughly between the end of Reconstruction (1877) under President Rutherford B. Hayes and President Woodrow Wilson's declared entrance into World War I, the United States' chief political goal in this period was to rebuild the South physically, politically, socially, and economically. Most white southerners viewed Reconstruction as a time "to put back the pieces so far as possible in the way they were in 1860, *status quo antebellum.*"[48] Consequently, the many assurances made during southern Reconstruction quickly gave way to a rebirth of white supremacist ideology and practice. With power given back to southern states at the end of Reconstruction, southern lawmakers moved swiftly to restrict the political and citizenship rights of Blacks.

The Dawn of the Black Clerico-Politician

Nevertheless, this period was monumental for Black Christians. Though Richard Allen and others had fueled the spirit of religious independence among Blacks in the late eighteenth century, it was after emancipation that Black Christians left white-run churches in droves to form their own churches in the South. That the so-called radical Reconstruction of the South gave Blacks, for a while, the opportunity to exercise political rights was a positive advancement. Altogether, sixteen African Americans served in the U.S. Congress during Reconstruction. For example, South Carolinian House Representative Richard Harvey Cain served in the 43rd and 45th Congresses. Cain attended Wilberforce University, the reputed "Black Athens," and served as pastor of a series of African Methodist churches. Interestingly, Cain's first pastoral assignment was to Missouri, a slave-holding state, and he next pastored a congregation in Iowa prior to ascending to the denomination's highest office of bishop. Astoundingly, Cain achieved clerical status as bishop in fourteen years. The politically involved Cain represents the model clerico-politician of his day.[49]

Others, such as former slave and Methodist minister and educator Hiram Rhoades Revels and Henry McNeal Turner, share similar profiles. Revels became the first African American in the U.S. Senate, and Turner was the Union Army's first Black chaplain as well as a member of the South Carolina legislature until Blacks were expelled in 1868. Turner would later become a high-profile bishop in African Methodism, and would rise as a leading national voice for Black emigration to Africa. Black ministers took active roles in Reconstruction politics despite their later exclusion from social and political power. These civic-minded persons ably served the African American community with distinction. Despite many progressive changes (creation of state-funded public schools, fairer tax system, outlawing discrimination on public transportation, and ending the death penalty) of biracial Republican coalitions in the U.S. Congress, southern Democrats opposed the very perception of "Negro Rule" in legislative politics.

Nevertheless, the Black church steadily grew not only because of the merger between the "invisible institution" of the South and the independent churches in the North, but also as a consequence of the emergence of indigenous Black preachers. Black clerics had been pastoring under restrictive slave conditions, but with the Civil War's end they were now free to practice their faith independently. Consequently, various poor, rural, mainly Baptist churches proliferated in the period, a phenomenon later analyzed and severely criticized in Benjamin Mays and Joseph Nicholson's landmark study, *The Negro's Church*.[50] Negatively, Blacks during the Reconstruction years were subject to all forms of violence and political disfranchisement. Black church leaders in the Nadir found the beginning of an increasing deradicalization of the church. While this did not mean political ineffectiveness, it did mean, however, that though the primary response to virulent racism came from the church, Black preachers would share leadership with prominent nonclerical figures such as Booker T. Washington, W. E. B. Du Bois, and Marcus Garvey.

The Reconstruction period was monumental for Black preaching and Black preachers in three ways. First, it had opened up opportunities for Black clergy to be bivocational. Bivocational status provided Black preachers an alternate platform outside the church to interpret and confront matters in the public sphere. Second, the proliferation of independent Black churches in the period created a cohesive structure for Black preachers to strengthen their bonds. After the family, Black churches were indeed the most important institution in African American communities. Furthermore, denominational conventions and associational gatherings became an important resource network for Black preachers on local, state, regional, and national levels. While most Black ministers were modestly educated if at all, as members of an elite religious fraternity having stake in the only profession open to African Americans, the period produced a more visible leadership model to aspiring Black clergy. Third, Black church deradicalization and the Black community's focus on racial uplift demanded that Black preachers begin to take into account the political dimensions of the gospel. Confronting social ills required collaboration with nonclerical secular leaders in African American communities.

Another key development in the period involved the preacher's recognition of how to counter the setbacks of the Nadir. Raboteau suggests that by no means were African American clergy unanimously submissive to the period's bleak horizon. The disappointments of the times drove many clergy to sustained theological reflection on the meaning of African American history as they sought to understand slavery, freedom, and oppression in light of Jesus Christ's witness. Though a few other important developments emerged in the period, Reconstruction was a disappointing period in the advancement of the human, economic, and social rights of Blacks in America.

The Great Migration Period

In the wake of the failure of Reconstruction, the rise of Jim Crow laws, and America's entry into World War I, the nation still found itself in a democratic contradiction: African Americans were still not free. Black lynchings were at an all-time high. Despite the proliferation of Black clergy-led independent Black churches in the rural and urban South, in the 1890s complex factors (i.e., agricultural depression, labor demands, and racism) combined to push poor Blacks into industrial centers.[51] Once in the urban environment, employment, poor housing, and overcrowding became foremost Black community concerns. But in these thoroughly congested ghettos, where a large Black proletariat was forming, it was impossible for Black clergy who preached the gospel from Sunday to Sunday to ignore the intense flood of Black migrants seeking refuge in Black churches.

Some of the large city churches, particularly those adopting an institutional model, not only proclaimed Christ-centered messages, they also developed social programs to assist migrants in finding jobs, housing, and basic education. While clearly a boom time in church memberships, not all northern Black congregations welcomed these southern Blacks into their fold. The tensions that class divisions posed within the Black religious community must not be understated. A clear hierarchy existed, especially between lighter-skinned and darker-skinned Blacks that created barriers to racial solidarity and cooperation. Class stratification or class differentiation among Blacks is an enduring reality.[52] This important development caused Black clergy and their mainstream Protestant churches to face head-on the basic challenge of yielding to a class-diverse southern migrant religious culture on the one hand, and on the other reassessing with new urgency the meaning of social service to the poor and needy.[53] However, positively, the Great Migration forced poor Blacks and the more affluent Blacks to relate to one another in these large churches.

Increased memberships in northern Black churches gave people the needed assurance of community, as well as strengthened the churches themselves. J. C. Austin and others skillfully organized lay ministries and auxiliaries within their robust congregations to attract and retain migrants who came from small church settings to the large urban churches. African Methodist Reverdy C. Ransom, Baptist J. Milton Waldron, Congregationalist H. H. Proctor in Atlanta, and Hutchens C. Bishop in New York were pastors of large city churches in the forefront of responding to the migration crisis. A religious explosion occurred in this period, and groups flowed into the Holiness and Pentecostal churches and the various cults that were spawning and multiplying during the war. Black Pentecostal preachers were developing new doctrines and incorporating them into a distinctive worship style and context, which uniquely distinguished them from mainline Black church congregants. C. H. Mason and C. P. Jones, who began to preach the Holiness doctrine of entire sanctification, were key figures.

The Pursuit of Human Dignity

Aroused by the discovery of the ways in which many migrants spoke with their feet despite their poverty and other vulnerabilities, Milton Sernett claims that Black Christian migrants in search of a promised land put their trust in the sovereignty of God to guide them out of their southern wilderness to the urban North. According to Sernett, the Great Migration was a religious event. Migrants transplanted in the urban North were carriers of culture who brought with them certain expectations about the movement of God. In the first place, a number of Blacks guarded their southern citizenship until crop-destroying boll weevils put in danger their basic survival. Many believed the disturbing presence of these insects was an act of divine intervention and a sign for them to take flight. Second, not all African American participants viewed their relocation to the industrial North in terms of the singular pursuit of material goods. But all participants, however, understood their sojourn as a quest for human dignity. Third, akin to the delightful word that announced the abolition of slavery at the Civil War's end, migrants had interpreted their escape from the South as the "Second Emancipation."[54]

African American ministers during the southern mass exodus were found at both ends of the spectrum. Some clergy were exodus enthusiasts while most were tide stemmers. That is, on the eve of the Great Migration, some southern Black pastors issued warnings to their congregations to seize the moment. Others, fearing membership drop-off, exhorted their flocks to "cast down their buckets in the South," discouraging northern flight.[55] It was not uncommon for southern Black pastors to receive letters from former parishioners transplanted to the North expressing regrets for not telling them about their hasty departure. Still, a sizeable percentage of southern rural pastors, in response to the migration's pull and impact on their memberships, packed up their possessions, abandoned their small churches, and headed north with their flock, hoping to reestablish congregational bonds in the northern metropolises. Sernett explains:

> Ministers who first opposed the migration, debating its merits with their elders and deacons, found it difficult to remain behind while leaders of their congregations packed up, often in great haste, to begin new lives in Chicago or some other northern industrial center. It was very difficult for preachers to voice reservations about the Great Migration over the opposition of laity who were staking everything on pursuing lives elsewhere.[56]

In accordance with such contrasting views among African American clergy, it is helpful to assess each in light of two important contextual considerations. First, the freedom to voice dissent actually depended on the circumstances of individual clergy. If one were a minister in a southern metropolitan environment, then typically one had more liberty than the country preacher to comment critically on the exodus.[57] Second, African American clergy were faced with the irony of white public officials urging Black patriotism for the war while countless Blacks were "being displaced from the farms and were without work in the cities."[58] African American clergy operated in a no-win situation due to the hypocrisy of whites. Black ministers recognized that while over thirty thousand Black men served overseas as combat troops during WWI, after fighting German soldiers in the cause of democracy, these men would return home to unfair treatment and pitiable economic opportunities. There were, however, a few Black preachers who were outspoken about this hypocrisy. From the pulpit and in the Black press, these preachers spoke in ardent opposition to an unprincipled democratic society that saw war as the protection of human freedom while it foreclosed on its own commitment to

Black soldiers returning home from the war. Northern Black clerics, specifically, were instrumental in the fight for human dignity while awaiting the return of Black soldiers to the home front.[59]

Few African American clergy in this period, even those moving to higher clerical rank from the small country churches to urban ones, revised their strategies to deal with the particular issues of the urban environment. In other words, infrastructural challenges were in tandem with theological ones. Like many of their white counterparts, the majority of Black preachers simply transferred old methods into new contexts.[60] Yet, preachers such as Reverdy C. Ransom, Florence Spearing Randolph, and Adam Clayton Powell Sr. were a representative Black clergy anomaly. They functioned as priests within their congregations and also preached prophetically to address the perplexing issues of their times, recognizing that the message of the gospel in a changing context necessitated fresh homiletical approaches, that is, new rather than old "wineskins." Their methods were not marked by migrant proselytizing, and these preachers did not comport themselves as labor agents or cultic gurus. Instead, "they were community activists," as Carol Marks correctly comments, "who functioned to stabilize the lives of the trusting and hopeful displaced, while simultaneously speaking de-stabilizing prophetic messages to structural realities that exacerbated the economic, social, and psychological problems migrants faced."[61] Within such a prism of social upheaval and progressivism, a few Black ministers emerged to fashion a distinctive preaching style—prophetic Black preaching—that challenged and expanded traditional preaching modes.

Ethos of Southern Black Preaching

Some ministers in the South preached patience and humility with whites, while others, regardless of region, demanded complete separation and expatriation from the dominant culture. This being the case, there were at least two leading discourse modes in Black churches that captured the hopeful imagination of Blacks bound for their promised land. The first is representative of the preaching of southern Black ministers who desired to curb migration fever. During the peak of the migration, acting at the behest of the white community, the Reverend Charles T. Walker of Georgia, one of the leading and perhaps "the greatest Negro preacher of the time," delivered sermons to dissuade Blacks from migrating north.

Migrant Thomas Watson Harvey explained that Walker's towering influence was incomparable:

> They called him the black Spurgeon, he was the biggest Negro preacher there was in the South at the time. And they gave him the courthouse every Sunday, to hold mass meetings and appeal to Negroes to stay home and don't go away. I remember they used to go to church. That was the only place a Negro had to go. If you didn't get it then you got it Sunday night. The preacher was always making it a point of duty to warn you not to leave. And they would go on and tell you how good the white folks was in the South . . . it was a general appeal. You got it every Sunday, you know. But that never stopped Negroes.[62]

Struck by the disruption of the mass exodus and Black resettlement and wishing to remain faithful to traditional preaching methods bequeathed from the Revival period, most Black Christian pastors, even the seemingly progressive and widely admired ones like Walker, in rural or urban settings put emphasis on moralistic concerns that gave primacy to spiritual formation over social criticism.

The second mode, spiritualistic preaching, which operated on different premises, came out of Black Spiritualist churches organized between 1915 and 1920. Seizing the sacred imagination of the interwar period, these congregations combined elements of Baptist, Holiness, and Pentecostal storefronts to those of Spiritualism.[63] As those prophesying in Corinth in the apostle Paul's day, mediums in Spiritual churches are believed to have the gift of prophecy in accordance with New Testament teachings.[64] Mother Leafy Anderson started the first Black Spiritualist church in New Orleans, but later founded the Eternal Life Christian Spiritualist Church in Chicago around 1918, where she headed up an association of Spiritualist congregations.[65] The focal point of spiritualistic worship is preaching, even though members do not appeal to a central organization per se to define its structural contents, beliefs, and practices. Typically, the pastor, a prominent member of the congregation, or a visiting preacher delivers the sermon. The preacher holds sway in the standard Sunday service or in special prophecy services, "usually from half an hour to over an hour in length; and in almost all cases is essentially extemporaneous" to relate and address socioeconomic and psychosocial problems. Naturally, preaching is done under the profession that the Holy Spirit takes complete control.[66] Many leaders in Spiritual churches claim the gift of divine healing and/or prophecy, though these gifts are not necessarily conjoined. Spiritualistic preaching possesses a strong disjunctive orientation toward the world. Spiritual religion substitutes religious status for social status. Not unlike many other Black congregations and sects, a person of humble standing may rise to the level of bishop, minister, or elder who can communicate with the spirit world. Hence, consistent with prophetic Black preaching the spiritualistic preacher did indeed seek to accord listeners a sense of recognition and dignity that would otherwise be absent in other social spheres.[67] However, due to its disjunctive approach to the physical world, spiritualistic preaching, at best, could only provide a channel for African Americans to cope with existing socioeconomic norms. The Great Migration landscape did indeed find a number of Black preachers invoking accommodative interpretations of the Bible as a means to encourage acquiescence to the status quo and discourage migration to the North. But the urban frontier also evidenced a wave of spiritualistic preaching of thaumaturgical techniques among the Black dispossessed, a message that in effect held that one could overcome personal and social problems by thinking positively.

The interwar period signified a time when countless Black religious leaders relied heavily on certain structural underpinnings of Black oral-based rhetoric. But recognizing first the particular influences American slavery and African culture have made on Black cultural communication is critical. Citing English professor Geneva Smitherman, Thurman Garner and Carolyn Calloway-Thomas notice that the core strength of the oral-discourse tradition that is so central to African American culture "lies in its capacity to accommodate new situations and changing realities."[68] Each generation and context may bend the tradition to adapt it to fit particular faith claims or ideological beliefs. Thus, one finds a range of Black religious discourse during the Great Migration, from Marcus Garvey's nationalistic message of the creation of an autonomous Black nation-state from the platform of his United Negro Improvement Association to Daddy Grace and Father Divine's unorthodox, personality-driven charismatic message formulations, displaying multiple temperaments and dissimilar objectives.

A final important advancement in the period is that many Black urban pastors found creative ways to respond to the Great Migration crisis by "facilitating a psychological space and opportunity for Black migrants to cast off Southern caste traditions."[69] Thus, they preached sermons that criticized injustice and emphasized the gospel's concern for all of human existence—body, soul, and spirit. In such preaching, needs were addressed, such as housing, jobs, and concerns relevant to daily living in light of the whole counsel of Scripture. Black preachers saw a more imminent need to promote a kingdom-of-God agenda, which related and appropriated the Christian faith in service to the physical and social needs of Blacks.

Civil Rights Period

By all accounts, the civil rights movement began roughly in 1954 after the landmark U.S. Supreme Court legal victory *Brown v. Board of Education of Topeka*. Thurgood Marshall and other legal strategists proved, in the Jim and Jane Crow segregation system, that separate facilities for Blacks and white were unequal in resources and Blacks were governmentally disenfranchised. Perhaps a more pivotal marker was the Montgomery, Alabama, Bus Boycott of 1955–56, a racial justice protest that brought seamstress Rosa Parks and twenty-six-year-old Baptist minister and PhD Martin Luther King Jr. to national attention. In the segregated South, Parks was arrested because she refused to move to the back of a bus, thereby relinquishing her seat to a white person who had boarded. Then King emerged. He was a skilled orator and preacher able to read the culture and with deft skill articulated both the lament and hope of Black people in an oppressive and violent social world. His preaching carried a sense of moral authority infused with a social justice agenda. Challenging the worth of an American democracy that racially and economically disenfranchised its African American citizenry, King, using Christian symbols and discourse in various settings, exposed the nation's hypocrisy and unwillingness to become a just society for all persons.

In the face of brutal racism and Jim Crow segregation in a racially rifted America, especially its most evident manifestations in the South, King and other African American ministers of the Baptist-led Southern Christian Leadership Council (SCLC), which King founded, effectively mobilized churches and African American clergy. King's SCLC had presence beyond the South, and the organization's strategic planning successfully struck a "happy balance between a [northern] bourgeois black social gospel tradition and the old-time religion founded in the slave quarters."[70]

Inspired by the life and philosophy of Mahatma Gandhi, the martyred King's vision strove for freedom through the ethic of love and nonviolence. "Nonviolence was not simply a political tactic, it was a way of life, the perfect method for translating Christian love into social action."[71] One critical component of his preaching was the will to speak the love and justice of God and hope for humankind in such a way that the heart of the oppressor would be transformed and the uplift of a wearied people would be actualized. A Baptist-bred, Walter Rauschenbusch devotee, King skillfully merged social activism with Christian ethics. It is important to note that not all African American clergy supported King's vision. The classic philosophical and theological squabble between King and J. H. Jackson, the celebrated preacher and president of the National Baptist Convention USA, is indicative of this reality. Jackson thought his own conservative stance concerning racial justice and uplift was more in keeping with the democratic ideals of the U.S. Constitution. King's protest strategy, Jackson thought, was too radical and would be counterproductive to African American social advancement. More than this, Malcolm X's tactics of "by any means necessary" to achieve freedom, including violence, in many ways countervailed the momentum of King's nonviolent passive-resistance method.

The increasing politicization of preachers was another huge development of the period. Based on the significant inroads made in the civil rights movement, religious leaders such as James Bevel, Jesse Jackson, Samuel "Billy" Kyles, Wyatt T. Walker, James Lawson, Fred Shuttlesworth, Otis Moss Jr., Joseph Lowery, and many other nonclerical leaders such as Diane Nash, John Lewis, and Andrew Young emerged to great prominence in the post–civil rights era. The politicization of the preacher's role as a defense strategy was clearly embodied in the Black preacher in this period. A more pronounced expectation of political activism and spiritual leadership became the self-identity of the Black preacher. The period drove many Blacks to theological schools to wrestle with questions surrounding race and divine intentionality. Systematic theologian James Cone's work is one example of scholarship that established a nomenclature to discuss theology in terms of Black racial and social identity in light of the gross neglect of justice and foundationalist views of white theology.

Despite progressive inroads, the creation of hierarchies among religious practitioners in African American churches during the 1950s and '60s created barriers to people coming to attend church. Even though Black churches remained the central institution of the African American community, leadership no longer fell exclusively to Black clergy; other professionals—teachers, doctors, lawyers—were drawn upon within African American communities for their expertise. Furthermore, Black clergy not only had to provide critical responses to the unyielding crises of economic and racial discrimination but had to confront a mounting academic revolution—evolution, biblical criticism, and secularism—that challenged the traditional faith of many Blacks. Another major development of the period was that for the wider society there existed real tensions within African American clergy leadership and secular leadership. The development of the Black preacher in this period displayed to the majority culture that there are and have always been diverse perspectives within the Black preaching traditions. African Americans in the civil rights period, particularly under King's leadership, demonstrated that faith could be taken to the streets and religion could have monumental influence in the public sphere. With the multivalent challenges facing African Americans, Blacks have benefited in significant ways from the role Black preachers and their churches have played in shaping the American religious landscape.

By tracing the origin and development of African American preaching and the African American preacher's significance in crucial periods of Black religious life, I have sought, in the main, to demonstrate and highlight key features that have contributed to the advancement of African American preaching and the religious formation of the African American preacher in the United States of America. However terse this tracing, one timeless description, though now over a century old, stills seems a generative and an appropriate depiction of the Black preacher's significance from slavery to contemporary times: "The preacher is the most unique personality developed by the Negro on American soil—a leader, politician, orator, 'boss', intriguer, idealist—all of these he is, and ever to the centre of a group of men, now twenty, now a thousand in number."[72]

3

The Trivocal Impulse: A Call for Holistic Preaching

A voice says, "Cry out!" And I said, "What shall I cry?"

—Isaiah 40:6a

Prophetic Black Preaching: Building Up, Tearing Down

Practical theology is a prophetic ministry of and for the church—and of and for society—when it interprets and acts, in the service of Jesus Christ, within human community toward the goal that Jacob Firet describes as the actualization and maintenance of the God and human relationship.[1] The common thread of all prophetic preaching is the recognition of injustice, and that the preacher will name injustice for what it is, and what justice should be. Thus, the prophetic witness is never imported; it is mediated, sent to, and worked out in community, not in isolation. In the book of Jeremiah, for example, the metaphors of prophet and priest are synthesized. On the one hand, in 6:1-6, just prior to Jeremiah's "Temple sermon" (7:1-15), Jeremiah, believing the Temple and its ritual practice were tools of social control,[2] exercises a prophetic function when he pronounces God's indictment upon "the shepherds [i.e., the religious and monarchial leadership] who have scattered the sheep" for their evil doings. On the other hand, the prophet exercises a priestly function as well, because, as Walter Brueggemann writes, he is nonetheless "called to be a child of the tradition, one who has taken it seriously in the shaping of his or her own field of perception and system of language."[3] From

57

his priestly pedigree[4] we may infer that his lineage afforded him a unique closeness to the tradition, especially the wisdom center of Temple worship.[5] Even if this closeness had only a rudimentary significance in the scope of the prophet's work, his cultural grooming shaped his worldview and thus, plausibly, provided him with the platform needed to preach his Temple sermon.

The Hebrew prophet Jeremiah is paradigmatic in that he receives an appointment from God to a work of "building up, and tearing down" (Jer. 1:10). Jeremiah and other biblical prophets were often called into community—a community that often stood against their work. Elijah hid in a cave fleeing Jezebel's wrath; Jonah rebelled against his assignment to Tarshish; and even Jeremiah lamented his struggle to Jerusalem. But without question, each prophet underwent transformation by virtue of his prophetic responsibility to the ongoing task of forming and reforming the communities into which he was sent. Jeremiah's life of service alongside the community, in which he was called, for example, was inseparable from his own spiritual process. And while not all prophecy was met with enthusiasm—for example, Daniel's interpretations for King Pelshazzar (Dan. 5:5—6:10) or Nathan's parable to David (2 Sam. 12:1-15)—the spoken Word is not conceived in, or directed to, or spoken in a vacuum.

More contemporarily, one might observe interwar-period America, when a distinctive form of prophetic preaching flowered in response to "the Great Migration," discussed in chapter 2, when as many as seven thousand southern Blacks left the South to relocate to the industrial North in search of a promised land.[6] The voice of the preacher was the chief responder to this mass migration to northern cities. In the midst of this social upheaval a few inspired northern Black urban pastors found creative ways to respond to the crisis, preaching sermons that criticized injustice, paired hope with circumstance, and addressed specific needs. Their preaching was fundamentally theo-rhetorical discourse about humanization. Specifically, they conveyed an outlook of divine intentionality that related to freedom and justice for all humankind. These few clergy where deeply devoted to holistic proclamation.

Preaching as practical theology carries a prophetic mandate. A practical theology that makes no attempt to work in the interest of forming and reforming communities, nor to struggle to emancipate the socially and economically crippled, and the spiritually oppressed voices on the margins, is, despite its good intentions, always impractical.

Priestly Black Preaching: Fostering Communal Trust

All authority in heaven and on earth has been given to me. Go therefore and make disciples of all nations, baptizing them in the name of the Father and of the Son and of the Holy Spirit . . .

—MATTHEW 28:18

Practical theology, at the same time, is a priestly work of and for the church and society. The nurturing and nourishing dynamics of the church's life must always be critically examined. Some churches die from cultivating attitudes and behaviors of apathetic resignation, that is, by neglecting the task of "building up and tearing down," which fosters the necessary bonds of priestly and prophetic witness. Other communities meagerly subsist, starved of any teleological aim, nonattentive to the wounded who desperately need soul care. The African American church, my own religious and cultural home, exemplifies why the priestly dimension is vital. Countless African American congregations experience a continual whirlwind of ecclesiological and organizational restructuring, essentially caught in a crisis of transition.

Many traditional and historic congregations founded and organized in urban or rural locales contend with the growing phenomenon of physical displacements, class division, and demographic shifts in neighborhoods. It is not uncommon to observe America's burgeoning Black middle class ritually commute into their urban churches for Sunday worship only to return straight away to their suburban quarters and corporate vocations, oblivious of the larger Black underclass in urban neighborhoods. As a consequence, this recent phenomenon tosses to the wind an infrastructure or tangible apparatus for building communal trust. Churches that exist exclusively as historical landmarks and spiritual fallout shelters, rather than as representatives of an active presence of God's gathered and missionally sent people, lose the ability to claim any strong connection to the communities into which they are called to serve, to their peril.

Moreover, many intimate and traditional African American churches are evolving into megachurches—a sprouting trend. Many Black megachurches, I find, too easily accommodate their charter and mission to the reigning "business-model" ideologies. They are less likely to be places that provide a sense of family and community, that is, of close-knit and supportive relationships for members. On the contrary, these houses of worship are primarily thought of as providers of religious goods and services to their constituents.[7] The ecclesiological questions in these transforming congregations are no longer exclusively based upon physical and spiritual survival as much as upon an emphasis on clarifying the vision and terms of corporate missional objectives. In what is clearly seen as a crisis of transition, the African American church stands at the precipice of dilemma and hope, asking: "Where do we go from here?," "What can we hold onto?," and "What do we as Black Christians theologically believe and adhere to?" Accordingly, this outlook creates fertile ground for priestly preaching. Generally, this crisis of transition has caused many Black preachers and their congregants to develop bifurcated identities: on the one hand, wanting to hold on to the folkways and mores of local traditions, and on the other hand, wanting to rethink and renegotiate congregational identity in ways that are technologically progressive, community focused, but in many cases nontraditional.[8] Bifurcated identities necessitate congregational strategies that reclaim and revise traditions and modes of religious practice.

Marvin McMickle's homiletic *Preaching to the Black Middle Class* addresses the issue of bifurcated identities. While centrally concerned with formulating practical ways to preach to African American churches, McMickle assesses demographic changes that point to an important and new ecclesiastical occurrence—the rising presence of professional-class Blacks occupying church pews. Importantly, McMickle challenges many of the outmoded congregational strategies for doing ministry in Black churches. However, though a provocative tone characterizes his preaching insights on the subject of racism, what he proposes does not provide an adequate remedy. He seemingly gives exclusive attention to the "priestly" dimension, one of Peter J. Paris's four ideal leadership types (1991), as an apt model to help middle-class Blacks cope and respond to the challenge of racism. Citing Paris, McMickle's preacher assumes the role of priest because "priests have helped the people to endure realities they cannot readily change and to make constructive use of every possible opportunity for self-development under the conditions of bondage."[9]

A valid recovery of the priestly function is desirable, indeed; however, in this homiletic McMickle ostensibly neglects the complementary role of the prophetic. In his more recent work *Where Have All the Prophets*

Gone? McMickle gives explicit attention to prophetic preaching and its importance in American society. Any polarizing resolution that privileges the priestly over the prophetic, predictably, fails to account for the ways in which Christian praxis, at every level, must hold the priestly and prophetic roles as indispensable to one another. Actually, as a ground for survival and social transformation, Paris better conceives the implications and nature of the priestly and prophetic dialectic when he writes: "The black Christian tradition has exercised both priestly and prophetic functions: the former aiding and abetting the race in its capacity to endure the effects of racism, the latter utilizing all available means to effect religious and moral reform in the society at large."[10] Only a reciprocally enriching prophetic and priestly conception of a practical theology for homiletics can bolster the health of the church's proclamation and through wisdom keep in motion the community's story.

A practical theology that makes no attempt to work in the direction of helping congregations negotiate faithful possibilities for creatively synthesizing their historical and ritual identities—while consciously reforming and affirming their charter in modern times—is always impractical.

Sagely Black Preaching: Enabling Conversation

> *"Let the days speak, and many years teach wisdom." But truly*
> *it is the spirit in a mortal . . . that makes for understanding.*
>
> —JOB 32:7-8

Practical theology is wisdom directed; it reflects on the past and present witness of the congregation's story in society. Making available the community's discourse, the preacher gathers up the artifacts, relevant concerns, and specific events in a particular congregation's life story and sets them in the larger drama of God's active presence in the world. The preacher retains a consecrated position—a set-apartness as the congregation's preacher, who preaches the gospel. But as homiletician Alyce McKenzie expresses, "a wisdom focus in preaching yields an egalitarian relationship between preacher and hearer that confers the same title upon both speaker and listener: sage."[11] In truth, the preacher is entrusted with the congregation's faith identity. In the act of proclamation the preacher as sage reminds believers of their commitments as redeemed persons who have declared allegiance to the crucified and risen sage—Jesus the Christ.[12]

One interesting and observable fact in Black urban and suburban congregations today is the adult church/youth church phenomenon—a separating out of generational groups during Sunday worship. Increasingly, on Sundays in many congregations parents and their children do not share the same worship space. Beyond the demarcating lines historically drawn at the church school or Sunday school hour children are frequently carted off to the nursery or "cry room" and youths are dismissed to receive their sermon from the often eager full-time, part-time, or volunteer minister. There are two venues for worship: (1) the large communal assembly meeting in the sanctuary, and the (2) children's ministry or youth church in another wing of the building. At some lulling point in the worship service, usually before the pastor stands to preach, the separation occurs. Prior to the young people emptying out of the sanctuary one might observe them being directed to gather at the church's altar to hear a children's message given by the pastor or some designee. This act functions, supposedly, to integrate the younger generation into the traditional worship format. But again, this is becoming less of the norm as youth ministers are brought on staff to conduct full services after a specified break during the general assembly worship time.

The separation format is generally welcomed by all. With children not strapped to the pew parents are free to focus in on certain elements of worship with minimal distractions. Such an accommodation holds great import for prospective members. Newcomers, especially with small children, make decisions about church membership based on something as simple as whether the church has resources in place for adults and children to worship in separate quarters. But for all its obvious merits, what are the consequences? In my judgment, there are just as many problems as there are benefits. First, given the departure from traditional formats, has adequate attention been given to the spiritual and economic costs accompanying such shifts? Smaller churches that cannot afford to pay a full-time, seminary-trained minister will certainly incur difficulty in retaining members. What are the repercussive effects of this phenomenon on the church's discipleship ministry or spiritual formation objectives? Is it not the case that church elders do a disservice to their important role as tradition keeper and mentor?

What is the appropriate point of transition? Does one go off to college and upon return find communal validations as adult worshiper? What is the role of sages if they infrequently visit youth church? Are college ministries to be proving grounds for faith formation, or are we gambling on the fact that our youth will link up with a "Bible-believing" community that will better prepare them for ministry in the public square? What is the church's long-term plan for a generationally integrated worship gathering? Is the waterway of shared wisdom dammed up because each group retreats to its own corner of the church? Is the youth pastor's vision in alignment with the senior pastor's? These questions and concerns, it seems to me, are worthwhile for any congregation to ponder.

The preacher as sage is called to interpret the causal and consequent effects of this generational splintering phenomenon. He or she must gather the community's concerns and self-understanding and ask the question: How must we do things here based on who we claim we are? Ironically, today, it seems the elders in emotively vibrant Black congregations do not hold as tightly on to ritualistic traditions as much as our younger generation hungers for innovation. Even still, both generations will fight for what they value. "The most salient division [in congregations]," says Penny Becker, "is not a liberal/conservative split, but a struggle between older and newer members to institutionalize their own set of values."[13] Black congregations today must pay attention to what happens over the long term when children are absent from the larger congregation's worship. What we do at church is not only expressive of our commitment to God through song, symbol, and so forth; what we do at church is formative and enduringly significant. Indeed, our participatory experiences will have implications for the future. Will an inclusive vision of worship that draws on the positives of generational inclusivity and diversity reemerge and be nurtured, or will the presently set nine-o'clock and eleven-o'clock worship trump any attempt to renegotiate how group worship might be formed?

In my view, each group stands much to gain from the other. If older believers are unable to access the knowledge of digital babies—the "texting" and "tweeting" generation—that Black church will inevitably fall off the cliff. Likewise, if young people lose connection with sages and elders, I am afraid that the increasingly irrelevant Black church will be, as religion scholar Eddie Glaude has suggested, dead as a doorknob.[14]

Perhaps the reality is this: since time moves on, all will be worshiping, young and old, in the "youth church," at least in terms of mind-set.

Three Contemporary Models of Practical Theology

To demonstrate what a recovery of African American preaching as theorhetorical discourse requires, this chapter offers a theoretically reconceived view of African American preaching by drawing on three contemporary models of interdisciplinary work widely recognized in the field of practical theology. First are the variants that the correlationists have offered, which assert that practical theology is genuinely constructive when theology and other disciplines are brought into a mutually influential dialogue. The *revised praxis correlational* model is an offshoot of Paul Tillich's method of correlation. Tillich argued that theology answers questions raised by the culture when the arts and sciences enter into dialogue. But more recently scholars such as David Tracy and Don Browning have proposed the *revised correlational* model, having suggested that Tillich's theological method is inadequate based on the view that theology and the arts and sciences should function on an equal plane. They ask: Why should theology have privilege over the human sciences? Still, Matthew Lamb and Rebecca Chopp further extend the correlational scheme with a *revised praxis* model, where the goals of social transformation are essential to forging a mutually influential, cross-disciplinary conversation between theology and the human sciences.

Second, like the correlationalists, the *transformational* model, first proposed by James F. Loder, claims that practical theology is constructively useful when theology and the human sciences dialogue with one another. Loder's model differs from those of the correlationists, however, in its assertion that practical theology is only true to its core principles when theology takes a leading role, which is to say that theology has at least a marginal priority over the human sciences in cross-disciplinary conversation.

Finally, philosophical theologian Wentzel van Huyssteen has proposed the *transversal* model. Of the three interdisciplinary models, the transversal is the most recent. Van Huyssteen claims that transversal dialogue is a conversation based on disciplinary intersections. Conceptually, practical theology closely identifies with conversation patterns that resemble an interactive network of several disciplines meeting at various intersecting points with the aim to yield fruitful theological reflection.[15] Because the transversal model assumes and heavily relies on a philosophical and rationalistic academic baseline that little relates to the goings on in the ecclesial practices of most African Americans, following the basic idea that practical theology is inherently an interdisciplinary dialogue, I draw into this conversation Dale Andrews's *Black church praxis-covenant* model.[16] In my judgment, one obtains a more full-bodied appreciation of the theological and ecclesial dynamics so central to African American Christian practice in general and African American preaching in specific using Andrews's practical theology insights.

Using these models I demonstrate how a reconsideration of their basic tenets mutually enriches one another and how, when drawn into creative dialogue, the tenets characterize how the prophetic, priestly, and sagely dynamics enable a constructive way of reconceiving preaching more holistically. *Trivocal preaching* is biblical, contextual, and catalytic. This being the case, its holistic impulse is perhaps its most notable feature. These interdisciplinary models for practical theology—when critically examined, dialectically related, and appropriated in and for praxis—can reveal a great deal about our theological understanding of African American preaching.

Interdisciplinarity: Implications for African American Preaching

Cry Out! Combating Dehumanization

Critical social theorist Matthew Lamb advocates fostering a mutually influential conversation between new social liberation movements and the Christian community—a conversation focused upon the *praxis* of each partner. Such praxis, broadly defined, is "the struggle against some concrete form of oppression and includes theoretical reflection that guides this struggle."[17] Interdisciplinary reflection begins, according to Lamb, when critical social theorists ask legitimate questions of theologies and ideologies. Lamb's influential text, *Solidarity with Victims* (1982), is grounded in the conviction that "the cries of the victims are the voice of God *(Vox victimarum vox Dei)*." His chief claim is that "the scandal of the Cross is the scandal of God identified with all the victims of history in the passion of Christ. That identification was not a passive acceptance of suffering but an overpowering transformation whereby the forces of death and evil were overcome through the resurrection."[18] Lamb's theory gives support to the African American preacher's understanding of what is at stake in preaching the gospel because it clearly articulates what it means to act justly in the here and now. More specifically, it enables persons to understand their situation in light of the justice of God and what God intends. Here we have the anthropocentric turn to humanity and a reference point to interpret the profitability of preaching in a socially unjust and violent world.

The critical aspect of Lamb's political theology is *agapic* praxis (self-transcending love that breaks the hold of bias on the human mind and heart) that finds correlation with *noetic* (intellectual) praxis. Accordingly, Lamb offers two fundamental claims. His first claim is that solidarity with the victims of history cannot be genuine if it (1) trivializes their histories of suffering by muting their cries and their claim on our consciences; or (2) seeks to distance itself from these histories of sufferings by switching places and victimizing the victors, thereby, ironically, making the violent bias of the victors its own. His second claim is that options for praxis that are open to genuine solidarity with the concrete histories of the suffering are, in fact, numerous, because of the pervasiveness of bias. The religious option is constituted in the conviction that to struggle for the realization of justice in history affirms that humankind is not simply on its own. Fundamentally, humans cannot justify themselves.

When Lamb claims that the cost of discipleship is to be prophetic through orthopraxy (right actions) informed by orthodoxy (right belief), then what we have is a critical insight into the social legitimization for the Black preacher to interpret the gospel with regard to justice ideals and the active practicing of hope toward emancipatory ends. In order for individuals to undergo genuine transformation of self by the gospel, the preacher of the spoken Word must first be self-critical about what following after Jesus involves. If the preacher is to respond justly upon hearing the cries of society's most marginalized citizens of the African American village, self-criticism is essential. That is why listening believers should employ a *hermeneutics of suspicion*. When religious practices under dominating pulpit authoritarians undermine Jesus' trivocal vision for Christian proclamation—proclaiming release to the captives and recovery of sight to the blind, to let the oppressed go free—Black preachers whom the community accords high authority can too easily fall into what Lamb refers to as *sacralism*. When God is identified in this way, "priests will protect—but for a price."[19] That is why there is an inimical relationship between sacralism and the sacralist bias. God becomes identified with the mighty and the powerful, not the victims.[20]

While much of what Lamb claims supports a critical recovery of the prophetic in religious practice, his revised praxis program stops short. First, Lamb too narrowly conceives of God's voice as merely the cries of victims. Is this the only image of God to be derived from Scripture? Conceiving God only this way fosters a disconnect between God on the ground and the Creator God who fashions the heavens and speaks all life into existence *ex nihilo*—out of nothing. Second, because Lamb does not seek a broad enough institutional base for his "new way of doing theology," its practical and constructive agendas are imbalanced, despite his program's strengths. Rather than enlisting local church communities and pastors as participant respondents to the question of what is at stake in religious practice, he only seeks collaboration with labor unions, secular racial and ethnic organizations, feminists, scientists, and academic theologians. And in his choice of academic theologians, he completely overlooks the serious liberation theological force in the works of James Cone.

However carefully one draws on the strength of Lamb's prophetic claims for developing a practical theological framework, a subsequent question must be asked of Lamb's practical theology: What comes after liberation? In the past, the traditional liberationists' responses to matters of spiritual oppression and humanity's redemption from corporeal sin against the Creator have been imperceptible or unsatisfactory. For this reason, James E. Loder's transformational model of interdisciplinary work, when held in dialectic tension with Lamb's insights, can give an intrinsic supplement to the prophetic claims of Lamb's model.

The Logic of the Spirit

Loder's transformational scheme presupposes that theology and its non-theological partners stand, conceptually, in an asymmetrical, bipolar relational unity. Christian unity is analogous to unity of the divine and human persons in Christ, according to Loder. Taking his cue from Karl Barth and his interpreters' reading of the divine-human relational dynamic, three key aspects are central to unity in Christ or the christological pattern.

They are *indissoluble differentiation, inseparable unity,* and *indestructible order.* As these aspects suggest, Jesus, the second person of the Trinity, is not simply a human being better than we are, having admirable and holy characteristics and divine attributes. Jesus, in fact, coexists with the Creator and Holy Spirit in a "self-involving" dynamic. The logic of the Spirit, therefore, is seeing Jesus in relation to the other persons of the Trinity in an undifferentiated way. To put it another way, there is no break or disruption of natures in the christological pattern.

For Loder, the divine exercises logical and ontological priority over our creaturely existence. This also implies that though the human sciences are taken seriously in the *transformational* model, theology is always in the driver's seat in interdisciplinary reflection.

Loder's "interdisciplinary and self-involving" methodology is important in our examination of the African American preacher's functional role as spokesperson of the gospel. A careful consideration of Loder that is critically examined, dialectically related, and appropriated in and for praxis reveals a priestly component of practical theological reflection on African American preaching that one cannot overlook. The priestly voice of Black preaching emphasizes the importance of justification, redemption, and sanctification in the life of believers, through Jesus Christ—the second person of the Trinity—and his atoning work. Consistent with the priestly voice proposed in this study, which emphasizes the sacramental mediation of Christ in preaching, Loder helps us to see why our justification, sanctification, and spiritual formation by Jesus Christ's atoning works matters in preaching since the believer's hope is so deeply connected to the transformative power of the spoken Word.

Transformation, according to Loder, has five core dimensions: historical, systematic, ecclesial, operational, and contextual.[21] The second, *systematic* dimension, is given methodological priority in Loder's program. With the person of Jesus Christ as described in the Chalcedonian formulation (that Jesus coexists with the Creator and Holy Spirit in a "self-involving" dynamic) as his starting point, one systematic task is "to point to the mystery of God's nature and action, organizing the human action disciplines in constructive relationship with theological disciplines."[22] In contrast to Lamb's revised praxis model, Loder claims that the baseline of a viable practical theological approach must be theological, not experiential, for if it is experience based, "the relationality may implicitly legitimate incoherence since it overtly rejects universals and affirms justice and narratives as universally applicable."[23]

Loder's program, carefully considered, helps the preacher to see the critical importance of the preacher's spiritual grounding as spokesperson of the Word. In proclaiming the gospel message in a way that is faithful to Jesus' inaugural vision, the preacher must do the work of calling to worship persons who are gathered in Christ's name; and, this, of course, carries with it the functional obligation of the preacher setting the tone. Furthermore, it is the work of priestly preaching to interpret and mediate the requirements of covenantal obligation to God and to God's people. To do this is to remind the people of God's faithfulness and promise keeping. In a word, the preacher's priestly voice is grounded in the recognition that there are no real substitutes for the "ministry of presence."

The transformational model is not without its limitations for doing theology contextually. For example, the slave preacher recognized the inadequacies of a "theology from above" that has formed the sacred imagination of much of Euro-American religious practice. By contrast, slave preachers gave greater emphasis to God who comes as Incarnate Word—Emmanuel—God with us. The vicissitudes encountered in slavery inspired the African to hold in tension both a "theology from above" and a "theology from below." Black preaching at its highest and best is contextual theo-rhetorical discourse that gathers up resources internal to Black life in the North American context. Structurally, the Loderian model is too university based, which corresponds rather closely to Lamb's noetic praxis. This means that Loder's structuralist framework relies too heavily on knowledge gained at an academic university rather than drawing from the formulations of indigenous theology in particular ecclesial communities. Granted, for Loder, proximate norms and goals are manifested in *koinonia* (fellowship of the saints). But according to Loder's program of relating theology and science to guide practical theological practice, practitioners, it appears, would need to possess a strong knowledge of theological themes and scientific terminology. Ironically, the theological conundrum here becomes one of access. What practical ways can this model be shared and implemented with the many rural and urban African American communities of faith who are often disconnected from cutting-edge academic resources? How could they effectively construct for themselves a bona fide theology consistent with Loder's transformational scheme?

Despite these limitations, the transformational model nevertheless offers the preacher-practical theologian a theologically robust model for conceptualizing the pattern of humanity's once-for-all and ongoing redemption. Regrettably, what remains underdeveloped, I think, is a discussion of how his proposed methodology could be refashioned to embody more fully the normative purposes of the Christian life in particular contexts of experience.

Notwithstanding the merit of Lamb's revised praxis correlational model for providing some inroad into the nature and function of the prophetic voice and Loder's transformational agenda that roughly speaks to a more priestly dynamic, both programs lack color, that is, context-specific content. Conceptually, we are implicitly encouraged to see and accept a doctrine of God and doctrine of the church with no feet in the world of racial/ethnic pluralism. We are not permitted to hear the prophetic and priestly soundings—the voice of the preacher and people—rehearsing the communal story, calling up the journeys of those exemplars of faith or how the stirring and chanting in the power of the Holy Spirit created frenzy and demonstrated the inexpressible nature of Black religious experience. The church was established by Jesus Christ, the disinherited one, who by salvation (bringing human beings into relationship with God and one another) and through adoption receives repentant sinners into familial relationship as a loving parent would a child. Relationships that are meaningful and lasting originate in places where people own a slice of God's story. Christ's church is a covenant community of gathered persons who by divine intent experience the core qualities of wisdom and faith in particular ways. No practical theological model to date articulates this better than Dale Andrews's Black church praxis-covenant project.

Refuge and Folk Religion

Dale Andrews develops an ecclesiological practical theology for Black churches. As a way to explore the role of faith claims in Black religious folk traditions, he reconsiders the meaning of survival in the Black church from slavery to present day. The question he raises is: Is Black church synonymous with political passivity and social regression? Andrews argues that the Black church has been unfairly burdened and branded by these descriptors, especially in the criticism of Black theologians. The

Black church, claims Andrews, has always been a *refuge*—a reservoir of communal care, religious formation, and liberating hope.

Andrews's theology focuses on the prophetic, priestly, and sagely dynamics of Black preaching and communal care of the congregation. Given his refuge conceptualization of the Black church, Andrews insists that "black theology's sweeping disparagement of the 'otherworldliness' of black churches indicates a misdiagnosis, which actually exposes a glaring 'missed-diagnosis'—American individualism," and thus has obscured the communal picture of the Black church's role and function in society.[24] Proponents of Black theology "have charged that black churches [have] abandoned their liberation history for an ineffectual spirituality, and therefore failed to confront adequately the concerns of black people living under racial and economic oppression,"[25] laments Andrews. These academics have (1) irresponsibly launched a liberation platform without the Black church's blessing—that is, they have abandoned the wisdom of the Black church and its sagely voice for the culture, and, accordingly, have tied their work to Eurocentric methods and secular Black power agendas; and (2) they have overlooked the vast opportunities to observe how liberation ethics, as described through the refuge paradigm, functions in the life of the church.[26]

Using the refuge metaphor, Andrews describes the functions within the life of the church, and attempts to make clear that the Black church does not promote escapism but, rather, is deeply committed to addressing the spiritual and material needs of its constituency in a dehumanizing world.[27] In terms of the Black congregation's social function and particular religious witness (faith identity), Andrews proposes a covenant model of Black ecclesiology that binds faith identity to prophetic reform of the church's communal and ministerial praxis. Four biblical tenets serve as guiding norms for a comprehensive model of ecclesiology for Black churches.

First, faith identity finds rooting in the doctrine of creation and concept of *imago Dei*. Creation describes the gracious and purposive acts of the Creator—the source of all created things—and functionally and relationally humans are to "image God." This insists that humans have a responsibility to God and an intrinsic worth to God.[28] Second, the development of faith identity in Black churches has traditionally invested symbolic significance in the exodus narrative. Conceptually, Israel's liberation saga in the book of Exodus legitimates God's will toward justice for humanity. No stronger biblical motif parallels with Black struggle in this country and will to overcome the oppressive forces against Black humanity.[29]

The third tenet tied to the development of faith identity focuses on the redemptive nature of the sufferings of Christ and the importance of conversion. Suffering is not an end but, rather, is "freedom from, or victory over, the ultimately destructive capacity of suffering or evil itself."[30] The conversion experience is deeply connected to the influences of Western evangelical Christianity, specifically its emphasis on personal piety and salvation through a personal relationship with Christ. The redeemed person is thought to be a participant in God's redemptive work in the world.[31] Lastly, eschatology and the kingdom of God bring these four tenets to a crown. Hope flows from Black eschatology. The fullness of God's salvific action displaces despair, and an anticipated future where liberation and reconciliation of humanity takes place is the highest ideal of this fourth dimension toward the development of faith identity. The sagely voice of the trivocal Black preacher gathers these elements of faith identity and names them hope.

Andrews's principal claim is that a chasm exists between Black church folk traditions and Black theology. According to him, this estrangement is caused, in large part, by the inducement of American individualism on Black churches, which undermines the communal spirit and genuine identity of Black Christians. "The chasm between black theology and black churches reflects the failure to create a counterhegemonic culture within black churches."[32] Black theology, Andrews claims, has been far too critical of the Black church's role in society. But is it not the case that Black theologians are right when they allege that Black church leaders today have abandoned their prophetic responsibilities in favor of a focus on religious piety and moralism?

For the African American preacher who would confer the community's wisdom and the wisdom of Scripture and inspire realistic hope for future generations, he or she must be homiletically prepared to preach trivocally—preaching from the three voices of prophet, priest, and sage. Hence, the covenant model of Black ecclesiology Andrews proposes is a critical insight into the reawakening and vitalization of the life of the religious community in society.[33] Such an ecclesiological framework, as Andrews claims, can bridge the chasm between Black theology and African American folk religion. In three ways the covenant model reorients and reestablishes the dialectic: (1) it provides for an interpretation of God's will and objectives as revealed in human community toward radical reform; (2) without equivocation, it insists that justice—social, cultural, political, and economic—be connected to the reformation process; and (3) it insists that the four tenets of faith identity—creation and *imago Dei*, the exodus narrative, the suffering of Jesus and conversion, and eschatology and the kingdom of God, which provide substance and shape to this ecclesial model—all converge to work toward the goal of radical reform and reconciliation between academic Black theology and Black religious folk life.[34]

What the Black church praxis-covenant model helps us to see is the vital importance of contextualization—taking culture and cultural change seriously. Though Andrews seeks to cull out a thoroughgoing prophetic practical theology, his ecclesiology, in my view, is an integration of all three voices. However, in my judgment it is the sagely oriented voice that is most pronounced. Set in a biblical, historical, sociocultural framework, this interdisciplinary model is about "community" and the shared work of preacher and community in reclaiming the Black church's communal, kinship identity.

Apart from the obvious advantages of thinking critically about what Black ecclesiology usefully offers Black Christians, the forward-reaching exploration of the state of African American preaching today is less attended to in this work. Andrews does not adequately discuss the widening chasm between contemporary Black congregations and the institutional practices and vision of the best of traditional Black folk religion, and how many Black congregations today are ill equipped and ill prepared to engage meaningfully some of the most complex issues of our times. How will the Black church and Black theology fare in postmodernity? While it is certainly the case that Black theologians must admit their failure to diagnose properly the true nature and actual inner workings of churches that operate and have operated as refuge stations, the Black church today must also confront its own failures to outline its vision for liberation and ministerial praxis for the twenty-first century.

Sagely African American folk religion declares to contemporary Black liberation theologians to first "learn the ropes" before making hard and fast determinations about the church's identity and obligation to society. When Black theology or any academic reflection on the Black church has the church as its point of departure, the one who interprets is better able to discern the interconnections between the refuge paradigm of communal care and concern for Black humanization and liberation ethics. To reestablish the discourse in this way is to form a holistic Black ecclesiology. A holistic Black ecclesiology beckons oppositional forces to come back into harmony to rediscover how the interrelationship between spiritual and historical liberation enriches the other and furnishes the common life of a particular worshiping community's wisdom and hope. In the end, the dialogical element of the Black church praxis-covenant model provides for what is, in effect, preacher/congregation egalitarianism. The implication, then, is that preaching's wisdom share is always dialogical. One of the gifts of folk religion is the sacred harmonies of "call and response."

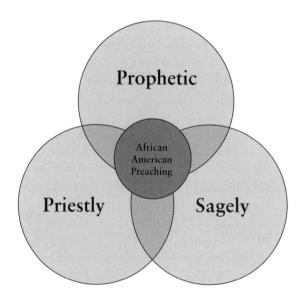

Figure 3.1 The Trivocal Preaching Paradigm

The Homiletical Upshot

Matthew Lamb's liberationist model stops short of this contextually robust presentation of the sagely dynamics of Black religious life and practice, and James Loder's transformational scheme carefully outlines the divine-human relation but seems to overlook the role of how contextually determined people work out their understanding of the incarnational presence of God in their midst. When Lamb, Loder, and Andrews are read and appropriated dialectically for thinking about African American preaching, creative dialogue can be fostered and Black preachers are provided a constructive paradigm to reconceive preaching more holistically. Taken together, they form a useful threefold cord for exploring synchronically the nature and function of African American preaching.

A critical appropriation of the rudiments of each—the revised praxis correlational, the transformational, and the Black church praxis-covenant interdisciplinary models—points the preacher as practical theologian toward a more authentic way of preaching and doing theology contextually. These models value the reflexive and introspective character of theory and the concrete realities of praxis in contemporary religious practice. Hence, an approach to homiletics that emphasizes the prophetic, priestly, and sagely voices is fertile ground for meaningfully addressing the state of health of the church's proclamation in our times. A biblically authorized confluence of the images of prophet, priest, and sage distinguishes the worth among the liberationists whose tendentious cry for justice and moral commitments demand more of preaching than Christ-centered sermons; it was Jesus who stood with scroll in hand in a Nazareth synagogue ordaining the prophetic work (Luke 4:16-20).

Today's preacher-prophet is consecrated to religious practice in the lineage of the biblical prophets and Jesus Christ; to the task of "telling again" the religious community to "pay attention"; to struggle against concrete forms of oppression; to critically theorize and hold theology accountable to its questions about justice, dominance, and freedom; to remind the academic elite of the ever-widening theory-constructing gap between the intellectually privileged and those on the margins; to rehearse in the minds of religious communities that Christian conversion demands a withdrawal from the sacralist bias that comes with orthodoxy without orthopraxy. And, even if prophetic preaching were to accomplish this aim, a true homiletic theology would then be only partly realized. Not until a critical correlation is made with the transformational model of interdisciplinarity and supported by a context-specific communal model of interdisciplinarity can preaching be, in reality, practical theology.

By establishing a constructive synchronization of these interdisciplinary models through these particular frameworks, holding in tension points of incongruence, the broad contours of what each interdisciplinary model proposes, at least conceptually, beckons the contemporary preacher as practical theologian back to the primary task of attentiveness, especially when our chief concern is the gospel.

A Homiletical Plan
for Recovering One's Voice

A sermon is a statement of faith, drawn from the context
of the tradition and projecting the authentic being of a preacher.

—MILES JEROME JONES[1]

Among a host of other physical health challenges, my father was plagued with deteriorating eyesight. Thus, he never preached from a full manuscript. Instead, the sermons he delivered from his wheelchair pulpit were guided by one page of notes scribbled on canary-yellow loose-leaf paper. My dad was an avid reader of sacred literature. He minored in religion at Baylor, the nation's largest Baptist university, and had planned to enter law school following graduation. However, these plans were sidelined after the onset of a series of health complications. Fortunately, he had some practical theological exposure, having taken all the Old and New Testament survey courses offered as well as electives in Christian ethics and Christian doctrine. Of course, perhaps equally important, having been raised in the Black evangelical Protestant tradition, my dad knew his way around the Bible.

Nonetheless, without a formal preaching course under his belt, his sermon preparation rituals were at best ad hoc. Unlike my students, he had never prepared a five-page exegesis report nor had he learned how to compose a written manuscript for a ten-minute sermon. These basic pulpit road maps I require in my introductory preaching course were not part of his sermon-creation method. My own homiletical outlook has broadened from bringing my observational insights from my church upbringing together with my more formal seminary instruction, where I learned to appreciate critical thinking about the sermon's development. My seminary training helped me to realize that if I were to preach in a variety of contexts, grow in the preaching life, and develop an effective preaching ministry, I needed more than congregational encouragement. The complimenting words, "I enjoyed your sermon," let me know that the sermon was meaningful to its hearer; however, such responses are not growth-inducing counsel. Obviously, the gospel we preach needs no improvements nor necessitates our human confirmation. However, a timely message prepared and rendered with a specific aim and logical flow is part of what it means to be a good steward of the Word and faithful to the task of honoring God and the people with our best offering.

Preachers benefit from constructive homiletical criticism. The evaluative response to a sermon by listeners is an invaluable gift to any preacher of the gospel. Whether that evaluation comes in the form of self-feedback, unceremonious roundtable discussion at coffee hour, in a review session with a teacher whose has made good use of audio or video recording, or through the sermon coaching of more veteran preachers who act as human guarantors for young pulpit novices in African American worship settings, the sermon feedback loop is absolutely critical to one's professional development.

Many African American seminarians of so-called free church traditions have alleged that their preaching classes at predominantly white theological schools offered them an unsatisfactory climate for "real" preaching. There is some truth behind their allegation. Although I had preached over a dozen sermons before entering seminary, I, too, felt out of place, intimidated by a new preaching environment. As one of three African Americans in a course of eighteen people, and the only one among the three with any preaching experience, I shared hardly any congregational experiences with most of my peers. This was culture shock even though I took some comfort from the presence of my two other African American colleagues who on my preaching days quietly whispered an "Amen" or two in support of my efforts.

Given my peculiar status as a licensed minister without the academy's theological certification, I had deep reservations about how this course would shape me. How could I possibly learn how to communicate the gospel effectively in a quiet, cold, sterile classroom? What could I meaningfully contribute? Why should I shoulder the burden to adjust to the prevailing Eurocentric preaching norms seemingly encouraged by whites who would shudder if given the opportunity to preach before an African American congregation? Would I start down the futile and isolating path of questioning the authenticity of my call to preach because preaching for me had preceded my formal theological education? What personal insecurities would surface in this academically critical space? Had I reached a fork in the road of my seminary experience, where the words, "Don't let seminary take your Jesus from you," had material significance? How could I return to my home church over the summer break without my sermons sounding pretentious to my listeners? I knew that words like "hermeneutics" or *homousious* or *perichoresis* wouldn't preach.

Given my limited exposure to and anecdotal knowledge of the Reformed theology that supported much of the preaching I heard in seminary, my early days in preaching class were bewildering. If preaching class could not help me relate any better to my people back home, then what was the point? Beyond the institutional stamp, I seriously questioned why I had come to seminary to learn how to preach. My appreciation for the course happened much later. By the end of the term, I learned that it was possible to preach the gospel meaningfully without feeling the burden to "whoop" and still be faithful to the wisdom and counsel of my ecclesial shaping in the African American church of my youth and respectful of those who encouraged me to go to seminary in the first place. Seminary taught me that homiletical criticism and theological reflection are beneficial to the preaching life. So I graduated with newfound appreciation and an added set of homiletical tools, but, more importantly, with a new outlook that would put me on a path to finding my authentic preaching voice.

Every preacher ought to have a reliable homiletical plan—a working methodology that enables him or her to contribute something of theological significance in the preaching moment. Without preparation there is no fitting and faithful speaking to one's community, and certainly not beyond its borders. No journeying preacher should be without a homiletical method for accomplishing specific preaching objectives. In this chapter I outline a homiletical plan for preparing preachers to preach *trivocally*—from the three voices of prophet, priest, and sage—and to think about preparing the sermon with an ear attentive to the needs, corporate concerns, and communal aspirations of people in search of a new hearing of the gospel, who simply want to understand better the sermon's purpose for their spiritual, social, and cultural selves. What follows is a sermon preparation strategy—a road map that encourages Black preachers not to abandon performative-stylistic preaching considerations but, rather, to add to them an avenue for envisioning the preaching task more holistically. *Trivocally conscious preaching* is absolutely crucial for communal restoration and revitalization of the life-project of African American churches and communities today.

Setting Up the Trivocal Sermon

A good sermon is a theological conversation about what it means to speak of a promise-bearing God who addresses the real needs of real people. Unlike any other discourse, sermons carry the potential to lift our one-dimensional lives Godward, says Samuel Proctor. A good sermon always "encourage[s] us to answer as we are addressed by God."[2]

The sermon can function in a number of ways that are largely "determined by the sermon's purpose" and the sacred text it considers and interprets.[3] David Bartlett lists eight possible functions. The sermon may function as (1) *kerygma* (proclamation); (2) *didache* (teaching); (3) *paraklesis* (meaning exhortation or comfort); (4) *anamnesis* (remembrance); (5) *makarism* (blessing); (6) *sophia* (wisdom); (7) *prophetiea* (prophecy); and (8) *parabole* (parable).[4] Despite these important functions, the most fundamental function of the sermon is to convey an outlook of divine purpose in a particular moment in time to a particular gathering of people. Therefore, as a matter of principle, in truth, (1) sermons preached have no shelf life and (2) no agenda except revealing God and what God expects in God's created world for a particular community for that day.

Sermons are not the possession of the preacher, expressed Henry Ward Beecher, but are "merely subordinate materials and instruments" dependent upon the living force of God, as revealed in Jesus Christ.[5] This is why the sermon's aim, in every respect, should be about revealing a clear portrait of Jesus and what it means to follow in the Master's steps. It is this age-old portrait of preaching that should navigate the preacher's preaching life. Sermons that convey an outlook of divine intentionality, I have argued, are necessarily tied to the prophetic, priestly, and sagely tasks of Christian proclamation: proclaiming release to the captives, recovery of sight to the blind, and liberty for the oppressed.

Spiritual preparation does not absolve the preacher from her or his responsibility to shape and contextually situate the sermon in the context of lived experience. He or she is entrusted with a content for which great care must be given to shaping into a sermon if the desired end of rendering a verdict that promotes life is to be achieved. For this reason, the preacher who understands that the "what," "why," and "how" components of preaching are never separable, and who is able to harness insights in regard to this mutually enriching interconnected dynamic, discovers a homiletical pathway to finding his or her trivocal preaching voice.

Before outlining a homiletical plan, let us consider again the principal marks of the prophetic, priestly, and sagely voices of African American preaching.

1. *The prophetic voice*—expresses unrelenting hope about God's activity to transform church and society in a present-future sense based on the principle of justice;
2. *The priestly voice*—encourages, through a variety of Christian practices, the Christian formation of listeners in order to enhance themselves morally and ethically; and
3. *The sagely voice*—confers the preacher and congregation's wisdom; daringly, it speaks within the context of radical social and ecclesial change for the purpose of keeping vital the congregation's vision and mission.

Rules of Art

In devising a trivocal homiletical plan one should consider four constructive tasks for preparing sermons. Each task assumes that the preacher first has a disciplined prayer life; a sense of call; a rudimentary knowledge of Scripture and Christian doctrine; confessional theological commitments; and a high appreciation for Christian worship.

Exploration

The first task is *exploration*. This is the information-gathering and listening stage of sermon preparation. The preacher begins by asking the question, What has driven me to the task of sermon preparation? Have I been brought to such preparation after some consideration or revelation in the biblical text first or in response to a rhetorical situation that requires urgent address? (We will come back to this momentarily). Following this are practical aspects, where the preacher asks: "What are the relevant concerns or felt needs of the congregation that must be addressed in the sermon and what will preparation informed by a specific occasion or ministry duty (e.g., a funeral, revival service, Mother's Day) entail?"

In this stage, a clear assessment of the rhetorical situation (public issue oriented or expressly ecclesially concerned) is a crucial first step. Lloyd F. Bitzer defines the term *rhetorical situation* as a combination of persons, events, objects, and relations presenting an actual problem, potential exigence, or an imperfection marked by urgency that can be radically transformed if the right discourse is fitly injected into and appropriated for the situation.[6] For our purposes, the radically transformative discourse would be the message of the gospel in spoken Word. If nothing of importance is identified that invites the sermon's address then the sermon becomes inconsequential.

For instance, one seldom-explored rhetorical situation associated with Black life in North America has to do with the perceptions and value-laden assumptions connected to African American women's hair-grooming rituals. Many would agree that beautifying one's appearance expresses love for self and some would argue that this is part and parcel of what it means to be a good steward of one's body as a creation of God. In too many cases, however, I suspect the range of cosmetic procedures to enhance one's appearance and the tendency to financially prioritize hair-maintenance practices over other life-sustaining practices of nutrition, exercise, or educational enrichment reveal certain pathologies and complexes African American women sometimes have about their appearance that their racial counterparts are less concerned about.

Beyond hair hygiene, for many women in the African American village, hair carries a sacred significance deeply connected to a woman's self-esteem and sense of being in a society where the Eurocentric standards of beauty are the most high ranking. For instance, little Black girls are encouraged to buy and model themselves after white or Black princess dolls with long, flowing, bone-straight hair. But in this seemingly trite example, a serious question must be raised: How does a Black Christian woman reconcile her own belief in the concept of *imago Dei*—the "image of God"—if she has become overly concerned or obsessed with self-beautification? Where does one draw the line? The line between care of self and love of self and self-hate is a thin one.

One might also point to the myriad problems Black boys without paternal involvement in their lives confront on a daily basis. Many of them despise their lot and develop wrong-headed ideas about what it means to be a man—engaging in irresponsible and self-destructive behavior such as the selling and use of illegal drugs, committing violence, and engaging in hypersexual activities that exploit and devalue Black women's bodies—that become markers of both status and self-worth. Clearly, the God who created us does not want us to hate ourselves. Self-hate undermines Christian hope and distorts our image of a God who loves God's own creation without condition.

African American preaching need not only be the fruit of biblical interpretation that addresses spiritual concerns. More than ever, preaching that demonstrates the importance of spiritual care linked to care of the body is needed in the African American village. Diabetes, hypertension, poor nutritional hygiene, and cancer are not only symptomatic of inadequate access to decent health care but symptomatic of bad theology and overspiritualizing. This is why African American preachers today would do well to explore the relationship between faith and medicine. Good exploration of the rhetorical situation allows the preacher to investigate topics and situations that are socioeconomic or overtly sociopolitical in nature.

Today's preacher must have something meaningful to say about global warming, poverty at home and abroad, sexual trafficking, childhood obesity, corporate greed, fiscal responsibility, the increasingly growing digital information gap in certain segments of African American communities, and the violence perpetrated against persons because of their gender or sexual orientation. As the world becomes smaller, brothers and sisters of African America, I believe, have a special obligation to be humanitarian and justice seeking. Part of what it means to be connected to a historically constructed African American community is to have some basic sensitivity to persons of African descent who suffer all forms of oppression and dehumanization around the globe. The preacher that fails to give both eye and ear to Scripture and flesh-and-blood human experience in the exploration task will never make a meaningful claim on the lives of Black people in a deathly world.

Consulting the biblical text at this precommentary exploration stage for a text's pearls of revelation and wisdom is a necessary first step in the sermon development process. Charles G. Adams has it right when he discusses this part of preparation. In the spirit of the sage, Adams comments: "In reading the text at the start of my preparation, I do not consult the commentaries—it is too soon to read the comments of others concerning the text. If God is speaking to me, I do not want to drown out God's new word to me by the voices of others. I want to preserve the fragile element of my own unique sensitivity to God and creativity."[7]

Whether the text is selected by the preacher or assigned from a lectionary resource, in the same way that one might ask questions and gather tools to interpret what is going in the rhetorical situation, the preacher must see that consulting the Scriptures is to obtain some footing into the world of the text by letting the words of the chosen pericope (unit of Scripture) speak on its own terms. The words of the text are not the only means for revealing the mind of Scripture, but the minutest of details or images that surface may lead the preacher toward a fertile field for a more intensive treatment in the subsequent clarification task. The preacher gets to know a text by developing a relationship with it. The preacher does not come to the text empty handed, but with a running script of thoughts, cares, concerns, biases, prejudices, and questions.

Fidelity to what is demanded of this information-gathering and listening stage is to find ways for this running human life script to have meaningful conversation with the biblical text. Early on, the preacher is looking for God to speak and to create a starting point for God and preacher to fuse the horizon of our inhabited world with the horizon of the world of the ancient text. But given the historical distance that exists between the postmodern preacher-interpreter from past events recorded in context-conditioned ancient texts, the wise exegete will exercise some suspicion of what the text may speak. Exploration moves the homiletical hermeneut to the clarification task to investigate further his or her own questions and suspicions, but primarily to see if there is more there than meets the eye.

Clarification

The second principal task is clarification. It intensifies the exploration. Following self-critical exegesis, the preacher-interpreter isolates a public issue or ecclesial concern and brings the rhetorical situation and selected Scripture into focus. The most important objective here is to move the preacher from rhetorical-situation assessment to the critical step of naming God's activity in Scripture and human experience and the gospel's concern for the community's care. The preacher-interpreter shapes the sermon's relevant concern, agenda, and projected aim. He or she then drafts a sermonic claim to be tested and revised later on in the homiletical plan as it continues to be shaped.

What will I say based on what I've seen, heard, and felt? What can be said in light of the goings-on in the world of the text and the world we presently inhabit? What must be said that only I can say? What does the text communicate about God? Is God angry and out of touch, or a close and trustworthy friend? How will the preacher name God at work in the life of the congregation? Will this be a message to challenge, instruct, encourage, exhort, rebuke, or some combination? The sermon's claim should have an answer to these questions. Marvin McMickle rightly argues that a clear and effective claim statement answers three important questions: the What?, So What?, and Now What? A good claim statement is a concise, compelling, biblically centered, and contextually relevant proposition. It communicates a central truth to be fleshed out and proclaimed in the sermon.[8] What he proposes in his short volume is of crucial importance as one moves from exploration to clarification and toward the third task—*internalization*.

In a trivocal plan, I advise preachers to write down two sermon claims but select one for the sermon to be preached. I suggest this for two reasons. First, exegetical reflection ought to have enough depth into the life-world of the text and the rhetorical situation that a multiplicity of solid and germinating ideas could potentially sprout. Second, for any given occasion the preacher may want to revisit the same pericope or segment of text in a neighboring verse or chapter to pursue in another direction. Biblical texts may supply a fecundity of meaning. The preacher runs the risk of reducing the text to one's ideological moorings if he or she does not take care to let the text speak beyond our fixed claims. Still, the text must be handled with care and approached with a hermeneutics of trust, not simply a hermeneutic of suspicion.

For this reason, deconstructionists make lousy practical theologians. Interpreting Scripture for preaching, by necessity, carries a constructivist aim in the end. As the ancients demonstrated their respect for the God of

THE JOURNEY AND PROMISE OF AFRICAN AMERICAN PREACHING

the text by handling midrashic texts to arrest their meaning potential, so must the contemporary cleric if sound theology is to emerge.[9] The more a preacher brings a critical eye when reading both text and situation, the more the preacher notices that some texts are not univocal (one voice). Every time we engage the text we come with new eyes, new questions, and new motivations from our ever-evolving selves.

In the three sample sermons that follow later in this chapter, the clarifying questions I bring to the text are: What must I say in light of my wrestling to understand text and situation? What hoped-for reality or outcome do I seek from the people I am addressing? Serious wrestling to clarify or bring into focus the central idea of the sermon for the people on a given day, for a specific occasion, at a particular time, I believe inches the preacher ever closer to obtaining a clearer portrait of the "kingdom of God" that he or she hopes will be revealed for the community's nourishment. It is in the task of clarification that the preacher isolates what can be said and what must be said.

Internalization

Sermon crafting and indwelling the sermon is an essential third step of sermon preparation. Some preachers want to skip the second step and jump to sermon composition. I require fresh sermons in my course. Each semester, it never fails, there arrives a student on his or her day to preach who has mismanaged the sermon prep time and now wants to submit a manuscript with no proof that any exegetical reflection was done. Skipping the exploration and clarification circumvents any plan to trumpet a certain sound, what Samuel Proctor calls crafting a sermon with authority.

Taking his cue from H. Grady Davis's *Design for Preaching*[10]—a widely used textbook published in the 1950s, which greatly influenced the course of contemporary homiletical thought and research—James Earl Massey, in his work *Designing the Sermon* (1980), convincingly argues that an effective sermon design will have "a point to make, an idea to express, a scene to share, a cause to promote, a doctrine to set forth and apply, an action to inspire, a feeling to arouse, a direction to point out, a divine promise to share, a caution to give, a person to claim."[11] Henry Mitchell helpfully notes that sermons should have rhetorical and emotive "build-up" that gets worshipers to celebration.

Reinforcing this claim, Frank Thomas reminds preachers that hearers remember what they have celebrated. When preachers take the time to design their sermons attentive to intuitive and emotive logic, a tangible, albeit mysterious, spiritual experience occurs in the preaching moment because the good news gets celebrated.[12] On different premises, William McClain adds that though there is always an element of hope in Black preaching, this preaching is characterized by its "matter of factness"; it is declarative more than suggestive. Black preaching steers clear of spurious sophistry and carries the burden to announce God's judgment on church and society.[13] Sorrow and celebration is the logic, of the Spirit in preaching because the Spirit manifests in the community's tears and joyous shouting.[14]

When possible the preacher should compose at least three sermon drafts. Draft one should focus on "getting it out" on paper and then "talking it through." The second draft calls for shaping the content. The preacher must write for the ear and the sermon's message must strive for simplicity and at the same time dig for the deep-laden pearls that emerge from the previous steps and that arise from the thinking and writing process itself. Finally, the third draft should have enough polish that it can be rehearsed and digested. The preacher should seek beauty of expression, relishing every word penned and settled on. After rehearsing the manuscript, the preacher should revisit the initial sermon claim to see if any slight revisions are needed.

Proclamation

Finally, the fourth and riskiest task is proclamation. After the exploration, clarification, and internalization tasks, the preacher now gives voice to what has been investigated, interpreted, crafted, and indwelled.

At this stage of the process the preacher, contends Thomas Long, moves from exegetical moorings (which are not inherently preachworthy) to actually announcing the sermon's claim on our lives.[15] Put a different way, the preacher does not preach exegesis. Rather, she or he now proclaims the gospel that has been informed by the exegetical process. The risk involved has everything to do with what the preacher speaks in the name of God. Unfortunately, for a variety of reasons, preachers may say inappropriate things, reveal too much of themselves, demonize folks in the congregation with whom he or she is involved in an unsettled dispute, or use the pulpit to spout bombast. Taking appropriate risks in the preaching moment should be Spirit-led. It should be about our letting God revise our manuscripts to speak a truer and more faithful expression of the good news even in the absence of a welcomed reception from the listener. The preacher's proclamation is healing balm, but it may also offend. The spoken Word possesses political power. It uproots and builds up; it always stands against something—sin, death, unrepentant hearts, and our protection and preservation of the status quo.

In the language-play of preaching as proclamation, says Teresa Fry Brown, "the preacher and congregation exchange faith talk in a give and take, call and response, verbal and nonverbal, vocal and nonvocal, and logical emotive manner."[16] The proclamatory task involves the unleashing of the gospel in the context of human community. Preaching that is faithful to Jesus' inaugural vision as recorded in Luke 4 is preaching that "proclaims release of the captives, recovery of sight to the blind, and letting the oppressed go free." Aside from John 3:16, there is, in my judgment, no clearer expression of God's love for humankind than what Jesus announces in this Lukan passage. I can argue this because in the announcement of the anointed One is also the declaration that Jesus himself is prepared to implement this announcement, atone for the world's sins, at the cost of his own life.

Christian proclamation is envisioning a God who comes near us and who chooses to show up in the preacher's voice. It is vocalizing human concern and claiming for the believer that the God who is proclaimed provides answers to life's manifold concerns. In Christian proclamation the preacher finds solace, challenge, inspiration, joy, and relief because the good news is always about life and victory over the grave. Proclamation of this kind sets up the preacher's field of vision and, when rightly owned, forms and reforms the preacher's self-identity.

A Homiletical Map of Four Tasks of Sermon Preparation

I have designed this homiletical plan for preparing preachers to think theologically and contextually in developing their sermons. The specific objectives outlined should be a preacher's conversation partner rather than a fixed formula. This sermon preparation strategy is a road map for assisting the preacher to envision the preaching task more holistically and self-critically. The hope is that over time the plan will become a sort of "cheat sheet," a quick reference (see the pocket map, in the appendices) rather than a tiring, step-by-step procedure. If African American preachers are to have their finger on the pulse of twenty-first-century life in America and be attentive to the needs, corporate concerns, and communal aspirations of people in search of a new hearing of the gospel, then he or she must have in hand a contextually appropriate, culturally relevant, and theologically informed method of sermon preparation.

Detailed Map

TASK 1: EXPLORATION

Information-gathering and listening stage.

1. What drives the preacher to sermon preparation?
   - What is the relevant concern or felt need?
   - What is the exigency to be confronted and transformed?
   - What is the specific occasion or ministry task? (e.g., funeral, church anniversary, Pentecost Sunday, Easter Sunday, wedding homily, youth conference, chapel service, revival service, ordination service, spiritual retreat, ministers' conference, prayer breakfast, Men's Day, Women's Day, Mother's Day, Father's Day, Martin L. King Jr. Day)

2. Who's driving and in what direction?
   - Biblical text →→→→ Rhetorical situation
   - Rhetorical situation →→→→ Biblical text
   - Special occasion →→→→ Biblical text or topic-theme
     a. Assess the rhetorical situation (public issue or ecclesial concern)
        — What is the actual or potential injustice, imperfection, defect, obstacle to be confronted that is affecting the health of the church and/or community?
        — What specific concern(s) can I identify as important and in need of address?

—What information is available? (e.g., scan newspapers, Internet, television, church business meeting notes, academic journals)

—What are the facts?

b. Consult the Scriptures

—What biblical text (s) have you selected? Is selection by preacher's choice or lectionary?

—Read and meditate on the text devotionally. Read it closely. Linger in the text.

—What details stand out or images surface early on?

—Paraphrase the text in your own words.

TASK 2: CLARIFICATION

Intensify exploration by isolating the rhetorical situation and biblical text to state a claim.

1. Self-critical exegesis (unmasking the interpreter)

   • What am I bringing to the rhetorical situation and biblical text?

   • Can I identify any causes that conflict with my willingness to confront the rhetorical situation or interrogate text?

   • How have I contributed to the criminal act of silence relative to a public issue and/or ecclesial concern?

   • How am I feeling? Tired? Depressed? Anxious? Excited? Offended? Indifferent? Clear-headed? Angry? Alert?

   • Take note of any changes in feeling and mood throughout process.

2. Biblical study through cultural window (exegetical clues and finds)

   • Scholarly engage the text using critical tools.

   • Wrestle out its meaning-potential.

3. Name it

   • What am I lamenting? What can I hope for? Where is God? And what is God actively doing in the text?

- Identify the fusion of horizon with the world of the text and the presently inhabited world.
- Can anything be celebrated in the focus passage? Is there an image, picture, or path pointing toward a just end or hopeful vision in or surrounding the focus passage?

4. Claim it
   - Test your exegetical reflections against the trivocal paradigm.
   - Do I sense a prophetic, priestly, or sagely voice leading and speaking as I listen to Scripture for its message intent in light of a relevant concern or felt need, special occasion, or ministry task?

5. Shape the claim (draft two prospective claim statements; select one)
   - What can I say? What must I say?

TASK 3: INTERNALIZATION

The preacher moves from exegetical reflection and issue clarification to the important step of sermon creation (crafting and indwelling the sermon).

1. Pair exegetical revelations with preacher's sacred imagination.

2. Determine movement: expository-deductive/inductive; narrative; mixed-narrative; three-point structure; Proctor's Hegelian dialectical; etc.

3. Form an outline (map it out).

4. Compose.
   a. Draft One—write it (get it out; talk it through).
   b. Draft Two—shape it (write for the ear; be simple, go deep).
   c. Draft Three—rehearse it (relish every word; seek beauty).

TASK 4: PROCLAMATION

This final task is the riskiest part of the process; after completing the exploration, clarification, and internalization tasks, the preacher now gives voice to what has been interpreted, crafted, and indwelled.

1. Give the vision voice (make it seen; get it said)

   - Pulpit presentation: Abandon manuscript, be guided by notes/ outline, or use full manuscript

     a. Seek freedom at sermon's opening and closing.
     b. Use of media to enhance presentation (e.g., laptop, Power-Point, PDAs, smart phones, other digital technology); experiment but be a technocrat (if it gets in the way of the gospel being proclaimed clearly, it must go or recede to background).
     c. Speak to shape consciousness; take appropriate risks.

        —Find the right pitch; establish a rhythm.
        —Offer hopeful symbols through descriptive images/illustrations (watch out for listener cues).
        —Value the moment (put the gospel in the best possible light).

2. Sermon critique

   - Did I abandon my claim?
   - Did I leave out important or unimportant information? Why did I leave information out of the sermon?
   - What voice seemed leading? Prophetic? Priestly? Sagely? Discuss.
   - How did sermon function? Was it kerygmatic, didactic, exhortative, blessing, reflective, or parabolic?
   - Did the sermon evoke call-and-response congregational participation; encourage contemplation; inspire sociopolitical action?
   - How did it play? What am I still hearing? Is there more to say?
   - What should have been left out altogether?
   - What did the people have to say? What did you hope they would say or not say?

- How am I feeling?
- Delivery and presence: eye contact, articulation, gesturing, logic, awkward pauses, etc.

Notes to self:

Three Examples of Trivocal Preaching

In this final segment, I lend my sermonic voice to this volume to illustrate how trivocal preaching might come to expression as a form of holistic Christian proclamation through the prophetic, priestly, and sagely voices of preaching. Using two sermons and an ordination charge I have delivered in different worship settings, I illustrate the trivocal paradigm at work. While for each I introduce the context and discuss the claim I make, I offer no homiletical analysis of my own materials. My hope is that the reader will overhear the elemental voices I have described in this book at work and get some sense of how these voices emerge and when they appear. Because sermons are oral-aural in nature and born in the congregation's interactions with them, what shows up on the written page does not always communicate the depth, dynamic, and other broadening dimensions of the sermonic moment. In my preaching I draw in a number of resources (matters of style—repetition, tonality, cadence, dramatic pause, etc.) internal to traditional and contemporary African American worship practices.

Therefore, I commend these written manuscripts as sermonic material with which to dialogue rather than to mimic. I seek not to micromanage your responsiveness to the written page, but to let you, the reader, interlope, imaginatively reflect, experience, and relate to the sermon's content in any manner you wish. As much as I would like to transport you back to the times and places they were preached, I cannot. Even audio recording could not do this in full effect. I do hope that these materials, in some meaningful way, speak to you and reveal something of my journey to discover my voice and the Christ-patterned vision that authenticates it. To revisit our sermon fragments is to be intentional about our pursuit to assess our ever-developing preaching life. I have suggested in this book that preaching around the scriptural images of prophet, priest, and sage helps the preacher to reassess his or her self-identity, to better evaluate and honor that which the preacher does—preach. What other means or measurement does the preacher have but her or his own reflecting back to see if what was communicated to self and others exercised faithfulness to Jesus' inaugural vision? Part of what it means to experience professional growth in ministry and be seen as one having a faithful and disciplined preaching ministry requires that the preacher be introspective and self-critical, making himself or herself vulnerable to the scrutiny of others about his or her work.

Sermon One: We Are "We's" First

People's Community Baptist Church, Silver Spring, Maryland
March 8, 2009

Sermon's Orientation

- *Rhetorical situation* (drives): Following the tragic death of Ms. Patricia Ann Simmons Kelly of Rockville, Maryland, who was fatally shot by her husband in a suburban African American congregation's church parking lot between the first and second Sunday worship services. Sermon preached at 8:00 A.M. worship service on the Sunday following Simmons's midweek funeral service.
- Second Testament (Gospel)
- Prophetic/priestly
- Narrative-expository

Claim: We live in a world of death-dealing circumstances that call us into spaces of deep lament, and which, for the hopeful, seem not to avail any tangible resources for sustaining our lives and confronting the fear of that last enemy to be defeated—death itself. When we recognize that our ultimate hope is in God, we can entrust our lives to Jesus knowing that his power overcomes the most perplexing of circumstance.

Text: John 11:17-39

Narrative theorists in the theological world are right when they suggest that human beings are intentional beings, which is to say that what human beings do and say becomes intelligible only when they are set within a context of what was before and what is to come. One scholar says, "We are not 'I's' who decide to identify with certain 'We's,' we are first of all 'we's' who discover our 'I's' by recognizing in others what is similar or what is different. In other words, we are not determined by biology, biography, accidents of birth, time, and place in which we live and by our past. We are what we have been made to be."[17] We are products of situatedness on life's continuum. Our lives are situated in a larger story.

The Akan of West Africa call this GYE NYAME, which means "creation dates back to time immemorial; no one lives who saw its beginning and no one will live to see its end, except God." We are caught up within a larger drama that began with God and will end with God. We, each of us, come to the human stage to play our respective parts. It is no accident that we are here. "We are what we have been made to be." We are products of situatedness and community. Martin Luther King Jr. put it so eloquently: "We are caught in an inescapable network of mutuality, tied in a single garment of destiny. Whatever affects one directly, affects all indirectly." We are "We's" first. President Obama sits in the White House because somehow or another he made "We" popular again. He did not get there saying, "Yes, I can." We are "We's" first . . . tied in a single garment of destiny . . . products of community . . . a part of the People's Community Church, where the highest attribute of community is attached to everything we say we are about. That is to say, "If one hurts, we all hurt." Tragedy, pain, and grief have touched this community with deafening intensity.

Somebody died here . . . on this property . . . in this city . . . of this county . . . of this state . . . of this nation . . . of this world. Somebody has been orphaned by this tragedy. I was not able to attend the Celebration of Life service this past Thursday for our dear sister who lost her life on this property. But let me say this. Part of my complacency about life left in the casket with her. Preacher, why are you bringing all of this up again? It is my job to remind the people of God that we are first "We's"—God's redeemed and being redeemed community that hurts when others hurt. The great accomplishment of the slave preacher was his ability to bend to the actual conditions of slave life and to transform himself into a teacher and moral guide with a responsibility to keep the people together at life's critical moments.

We do not pray for Pastor Robinson and his family because we want to hear a good sermon every time we come through those doors. We pray for him because he has the unenviable task of keeping the people together, encouraging faith and fortitude, when complex problems yield no easy answers. Pain and grief are the headliners in this eleventh chapter of John. I want to invite your attention now to a familiar story that I hope will have new meaning for us today. It reads:

> When Jesus arrived, he found that Lazarus had already been in the tomb for four days. Now Bethany was near Jerusalem, some two miles away, and many of the Jews had come to Martha and Mary to console them about their brother. When Martha heard that Jesus was coming, she went and met him, while Mary stayed at home. Martha said to Jesus, "Lord, if you had been here, my brother would not have died. But even now I know that God will give you whatever you ask of him." Jesus said to her, "Your brother will rise again." Martha said to him, "I know that he will rise again in the resurrection on the last day." Jesus said to her, "I am the resurrection and the life. Those who believe in me, even though they die, will live, and everyone who lives and believes in me will never die. Do you believe this?" She said to him, "Yes, Lord, I believe that you are the Messiah, the Son of God, the one coming into the world."

They had stones in hand. They pressed him, "If you are the Messiah, tell us straight up." "I do the work of my Father . . . my Father . . . my Father and I are one . . . and still you do not believe," Jesus says. And so, they took up stones to stone him. Then they tried to arrest him, but he escaped from their hands. They took up stones to kill him. Jesus abandons safety from imminent death to respond to a death that put a community in crisis. Two sisters sent a message to him that compelled him to go back to the place where those Jewish authorities threatened to stone him. "Teacher, don't you know it is not safe to go back?" . . . his disciples say to him. "Our friend Lazarus has fallen asleep, I am going there to wake him up." Asleep. "If he has fallen asleep, he will be alright." Jesus said to them: "Lazarus is dead." Our friend Lazarus, our dear brother, was ill and has died. I must go back.

By the time he arrives in Bethany his friend Lazarus's body had been sitting in the tomb four days.

Death had come to the community and there was no recovery plan. There at center stage are two grieving sisters who have buried their brother Lazarus. A family and community mourns for the deceased, and the only viable hope in the time of desperation is delayed. Not there, they said, when he was supposed to be. Jesus is late, at least according to the community's calculations. To a family whom he loved so dearly, his absence, it seemed, was not congruent with his known compassion. The sisters of Lazarus sent word for Jesus without knowing that their faith would be put to the test.

Mary and Martha, these two sisters. Both had uncommon love for their brother Lazarus. And despite the death of their ill brother, these sisters had remained hopeful that Lazarus would be healed of his infirmity and live. What gave them hope was the fact that Jesus was near, and they felt that all they needed to do was "call him" and "tell him" what they wanted him to do. The nearness of Jesus nourished their faith. But their faith took a dip when Jesus' arrival on the scene was delayed. Ultimately, their urgent cries became cries of doubt and fear rather than faith. When we see things getting so bad around us discouragement is not far. When the nearness of God is not enough to comfort us, to calm our anxieties, our faith has taken a dip, and discouragement is not far.

But what this narrative is time-tested to teach us is that the tears of a lamenting community are not off the radar of God's concern. Such a portrait of these forlorn sisters brings to mind that Negro spiritual "O Mary Don't You Weep," tell "Martha not to moan." One weeps, the other moans . . . both are hurting. They've lost something, someone they once had. "O Mary don't you weep, tell Martha not to moan" is not to shush the one grieving. Here, it is not that weeping is impermissible in tragic times but, rather, it suggests getting it out, owning up to the fact that you are hurting, lamenting loss. Weeping and moaning may very well be the gateway for you to hope. Mary should not weep as one without hope. If God could liberate the Hebrews from their oppressive situation, then mourning and weeping, as the song continues, is chastened by the consolation that victory is the prize of the Hebrews because "Pharaoh's army got drowned in the Red Sea."[18] O Mary, O Mary, O Mary . . . Pharoah's army got drowned in the Red Sea.

To read John 11 is to see that we are invited to find our own story within these pages of Scripture, for who has not become personally acquainted with sickness and despair or known of someone who has? The hard facts are laid out in earlier verses of this chapter: "Lazarus is dead!" Martha and Mary were aware of this. Death's sting became a troubler of faith. Even those who had traveled with Jesus the miracle worker—the same Jesus who honored blind Bartimaeus's request to see, the same Jesus who honored a paralytic's desire to walk again, the same

Jesus whose cloak was good enough to satisfy a hemorrhaging woman's thirst for wellness, Jesus . . . not too busy to hear a synagogue ruler's petition for the restored life of his young child. Those who traveled with him were among the disbelieving in need of proof.

When Jesus spoke to the disciples he was deeply vexed, but when he encountered Mary weeping, he was deeply moved. His compassion met Mary's despondency. Her hurt, hurt him. Her inability to pull it together moved him. I don't know if he gave her a hug, a look, a towel. He was deeply moved. His compassion for her was greater than her inability to pull it together. So the question is not whether Jesus responds to our ignorance or points of despair. The question this text engenders is this: Under what authority do dead things come back to life and why must faith be jolted by sign?

The story is parabolic. A lesson follows the miracle demonstrated. Stones that block the flow of life and frustrate God's healing fount are taken away at Jesus' word. "Take away the stone . . . Lazarus, come out!"

In our culture of death-dealing circumstances and despair, individuals require more than what professional help and New Age spirituality can offer. While these accepted aspects for nurturing well-being may support the maintenance of physical and emotional health, in the end, they are no substitute for believing faith. If the nondiscriminating forces of death and despair are the last enemies to be overcome, then Jesus, life's healing balm, must be sought to win the war. When we see things getting so bad around us discouragement is not far.

My own period of doubt and fear came crashing in due to the fact that I did not mourn my father's death appropriately. He died at fifty years of age, when I had just begun college. Fifteen years later, I have found that coping with the reality of his death has been the most unsettled aspect of my life. Emotional healing is what I needed. To acknowledge now the work of God in my healing process has transformed my forward movement in faith; through our search for healing we encounter the spiritual presence of God that overturns our fears. Henri Nouwen's classic *The Wounded Healer* has rightly claimed that while even ministers are wounded, their wound might very well inspire a resurrected faith.

This text points . . . after Lazarus is resurrected Mary anoints Jesus' feet, the chief priests plot to do away with Lazarus, the resurrected one.

Jesus rides into Jerusalem on a borrowed colt and then he washes the feet of his disciples. Peter denies him. He is betrayed by a kiss. Taken to the high priest. Peter denies him again. He is interrogated by the chief priests. Peter denies him again. Pilate finds no fault but the people win out. Jesus is sentenced to death. He is crucified.

This text points . . . the overarching beauty of this text . . . dead things live again. There is a pregnant pause in the narrative . . . for if one continues on reading one sees that cries in Bethany give way to wailing in Gethsemane . . . and wailing in this dark garden ushers us into a violent mob who would only be satisfied with a cross-hung, broken, and bloodied body. Death-dealing circumstances are nailed there . . . Calvary . . . lies and deceit . . . nailed there . . . heartache and pain . . . nailed there . . . poverty and sickness . . . nailed there . . . every burden, every care . . . nailed down, tacked down . . . at Calvary. The violent mob would not be satisfied. They demanded blood! Living things die just as dead things live.

Another tomb. This one empty. Mary Magdalene and Mary preached the gospel first . . . the text claims that they saw the stone rolled away from the tomb. Simon Peter confirms. The linen wrappings lying there, the cloth that had been on Jesus' head, not lying with the linen wrappings but rolled up in a place by itself.

Stones get taken away. Death is defeated. Victory comes.

Sermon Two: The Ministry of the Towel

Michigan Park Christian Church, Washington, D.C.
June 14, 2009

Sermonic Orientation

- *Special occasion (drives)*: Ordination charge to former student, the Reverend Toni Ross
- Sagely
- Topical-thematic

Claim: Faithfulness to ministry requires that we be servant-leaders. When we honor God in our service to others we discover a divine validation and find grace to perform our work.

I must say to you on this momentous occasion of commissioning that this service was arranged long before you knew a day like this would come. The bulletins were already printed, program participants had instructions already in hand, and guests invited to celebrate with you were already scheduled to come. This is a providential moment. A moment already provided for and to which you have been catching up.

"Before I formed you in the womb I knew you, and before you were born I consecrated you." God has been at work in your life, and it goes without saying that you, a minister of the gospel, should so live as to bring honor to the vocation of ministry in your love and obedience to God and in your service to others.

Having accepted God's call to leadership in Christ's church and/or to the ordained work of specialized ministry, you covenant with God to serve Christ and the people of God with God's help, to deepen your obedience to the two great commandments: love the Lord your God with all your heart, soul, mind, and strength, and love your neighbor as yourself.

To love God, self, and neighbor exacts a cost. The call to discipleship is a summoning to all who would dare to follow, that is, to come and die. Not only dying to self, but being willing to take up life's crosses to follow Jesus. And, to follow him is to be in alignment with what God is doing in the world. Through your ministry God will draw others to God's own heart.

Therefore, let Jesus be your great example of a disciplined ministry. Beyond the titles you will assume from this day forward, REVEREND, RIGHT REVEREND, THE MOST RIGHT REVEREND, your first ministry is the ministry of the towel. "Then Jesus poured water into a basin and began to wash the disciple's feet and to wipe them with a towel that was tied around him." Let it be said that Toni Ross has a disciplined ministry, that she has a Bible in one hand and a towel in the other.

And so, having accepted God's call to ordained ministry: Will you continue to demonstrate your love and personal commitment for God as revealed in Jesus Christ? Will you speak truth to power both within and without the sanctuary's walls? Will you hold the hands of the bereaved, pray for the sick, help the poor and needy, visit those who are held captive, and care for all others who suffer on the margins of our society? Will you strive together with other colleagues in ministry to preserve the dignity, maintain the discipline, and promote the integrity of the vocation to which you have been called?

I charge you now to go forth with fear and trembling, with faith and assurance, with the love for justice and peace, but most of all, go forth in the power of Almighty God.

Sermon Three: We Have This Ministry

Howard University School of Divinity, Thurman Chapel
September 15, 2010

Sermon's Orientation

- *Special occasion (drives)*: "Pinning Ceremony" for new entrants and returning students
- Prophetic/Priestly/Sagely (Trivocal)
- Traditional-Narrative (Mixed)

Claim: Despite the deathly reality that confronts us all in this context of human suffering, we who are preparing for ministry in the postmodern world must find the courage to reclaim an assertive yet tensive posture of Christian confession without being defensive or arrogant. When we share our pain and difficult life experiences with God and others, we can be assured that our theological preparations for ministry will be life changing and consequential.

Text: Romans 4:18—5:5

The Ministry of Pain

For most parents, joy is experienced when a new baby comes into the world; it is experienced when we are celebrated for some act or applauded for some good work we have done.

Joy and pride fill our hearts when what we have spoken to another evokes laughter or wins a smile. Or, when we have made a promise and kept it. We experience joy. We feel good about ourselves.

To know that our sacrifices are appreciated at home, on our jobs; that we are loved by our family and friends is to experience true joy. We experience great pleasure when all is well, and when we know that the gift of love is in our possession.

But what about pain? What about the hardships life so often brings? What about the things that makes us so miserable at times . . . the joy robbers, the daily annoyances, the unforeseen betrayals of our trust, the unanticipated loss of work and income . . . things that suck the beauty out of life . . . the negatives of our existence that make us bow to them humbly?

When I was a little boy growing up in Waco, Texas, I did not understand why my father, who is now deceased, would visit the sick and shut-in at their homes or in the hospital or convalescent care facility, when he himself was chronically ill. He was a small-city pastor who could not walk. He led a five-hundred member congregation from his wheelchair pulpit.

I cannot remember a day when he was not in pain—not a single day could he forgo his medication ritual and enjoy freedom from the ailments that afflicted him so. What I know about crosses is what I had eyewitnessed day after day. Whether bathing him, dressing him, preparing his food, holding a cup to his mouth to drink, lifting him in and out of his wheelchair, as young boy, *I learned to respect the crosses people bear.*

Howard Thurman once said, "there is a ministry of pain."[19] I know this to be true. There is a ministry of pain. A ministry where one's healing may be found in the fellowship of those who suffer. We'd go with him, after church or during the midweek, to visit his parishioners in their homes or in hospitals. Driving from house to house; steering his wheelchair from room to room.

Those persons he would visit seemed to light up upon hearing his voice. Shouldering unbearable pain himself, he'd say, "How are you feeling today?" Most times the same question was posed to him, "Pastor, how are you feeling today?"

The authenticity of this exchange taught me something. "Your pain is not just your pain." Your pain is to be distributed throughout the body—the body of Christ. These exchanges taught me the beauty of fellowship.

Fellowship. Shared suffering. Bringing our pains to God together.

God had orchestrated it so that my father's own healing of the soul was deeply connected to his capacity and commitment to share in the suffering of others. Henri Nouwen calls this wounded healing. Nouwen argues that ministers are called to identify the suffering in their own lives and make that recognition the starting point of service. When we ministers leave ourselves open to others as co-sufferers, having the same wounds as those we serve, *we heal from our wounds.*[20] That is why sharing our pain is important.

Our pain can be a ministry. Therefore, it is important to recognize, given the fact that we all experience pain, that it is possible for us to make pain contribute to the health of our souls, the renewing of our faith . . . to the meaning and vitality of our lives.

There is a ministry of pain. A consequential ministry. A ministry where we ourselves might find healing balm. There is a ministry in our suffering if we can find an avenue of grace. In our compassion for others . . . we may indeed anticipate and find that our own strength is renewed.

Dedication to the cause of Christ is first a ministry of pain.

Lutheran pastor-theologian and martyr Dietrich Bonhoeffer once said, *"The cross is laid on every Christian."*[21] Life's difficulties help us to *revise our outdated maps . . . our outmoded views of reality that we so desperately and actively cling to.*[22]

The cross rubs up against us to rob us of our *totalizing self-sufficiency*, our *rugged individualism*, and demands that we know the difference that "faith in God" makes in this life. Dedication to the cause of Christ is a ministry of pain.

The Ministry of Grace

Therefore, since we are justified by faith—sinners declared "just" on the basis of the righteousness of God—redemption is possible. For the faithful there often appears a redemptive quality associated with the ministry of pain. Redemptive because it is often in our pain that we become aware, acquainted with the grace of God. For those who believe in the grace of God made possible through Jesus Christ, suffering can be redemptive. Suffering does not get the best of us . . . it does not kill our souls. We are the people of God. And since we belong to God . . . we belong to grace . . . and because those of us who believe in the Lord Jesus Christ are justified by faith . . . it is through him that we have access to the ministry of grace.

In their quest to understand the mystery of God's grace, over the centuries theologians have sought to describe this mystery. Some distinctions have been made in reference to grace. There is grace that is common; grace that is saving; grace that is prevenient; and grace that is sanctifying.

Common grace is indiscriminate favor; it does not matter who you are . . . it is universal; you are a recipient of the blessings of rain and sunshine like everybody else. Saved or not.

It is, however, not the grace that removes the penalty of sin . . . saving grace does that. Saving grace is what releases us from guilt and shame and changes our inner life. Saving grace is once-I-was-lost-but-now-I-am-found, was-blind-but-now-I-see grace. Common grace prepares the sinner to be receptive to the saving grace.

Then there is prevenient grace. Prevenient grace is God's provision for you before you are aware of it. It is grace in front of you that you have not caught up with yet. And finally, sanctifying grace. Sanctifying grace is the grace of consecration . . . grace that sets you apart for God's special use.

There is a ministry of pain in the life of a Christian, and pain has its place. Likewise there is a place for grace. In the sphere of God's love, it is true that we cannot escape pain. But it is also true that we cannot escape grace. That's the paradox. The pain of death is what we see at the foot of the cross . . . the fulfillment of grace is on the other side of the empty tomb.

This is at the heart of our Christian confession!

I played high school football. Life would have it that I would have my share of good and bad coaches. The good ones never let me quit. The bad ones never let me play.

Every coach had a play book . . . a whistle . . . and a speech. Sometimes the play book worked . . . most times it did not . . . sometimes the whistle worked . . . occasionally it had no effect . . . sometimes a motivational speech was all that was needed . . . But no pep talk mattered if the players were not willing to stick it out. Focus! Keep your head in the game!

When the beauty of life is sucked out that's when our faith needs a "pep talk."

We must take care not to reduce the life of a Christian to a game. Life is not a game; it is much more. Games have an end to them that human preparation can shape and often determine. Not so with life; life is not a game, life is a gift . . . a gift of grace.

Paul lifts up themes of certainty and expectancy in this text. In verse 18 of that fourth chapter, it reads, "Hoping against hope, Abraham believed he would become 'the father of many nations.' He did not weaken in faith when he considered his own body, which was already as good as dead. . . . [but he was] fully convinced that God was able to do what God had promised. Therefore his faith was credited to him as righteousness."

Look at what this text is doing. Paul mines the hermeneutical gap . . . he explodes the ideational meaning of the text . . . in Paul's hands the story of Abraham is not some fixed, musty mystery of days long ago. Rather, as he sees it, Abraham's faith extends a legacy privilege. But the Scripture that says "it was credited to him" was not written only for Abraham's sake. It was written for the Gentiles and Jews . . . for us. Those of us who dare to believe in the one who raised Jesus our Lord from the dead. Who was handed over for our misdeeds and mistakes, and was raised to meet the requirements of righteousness for us.

Now we can have a robust intellectual discussion about how his work on the cross met the requirements of righteousness for us. We might appeal to St. Anselm's atonement theory of satisfaction, that Jesus met the requirements of divine justice and thus the sinner's penalty satisfied. Or Gustav Aulén's view that the saving significance of Jesus' death is grounded in a theory of ransom . . . the requirements were met because Jesus claimed the keys to set the captives free . . . to deliver those who languish imprisoned by oppressive circumstances. We might even theorize about the carpenter's son meeting the requirements of righteousness for us by virtue of moral influence, that is, Jesus' death on the cross draws us to God by a profound demonstration of divine love.[23]

However one comes out, be it *satisfaction, ransom,* or *moral influence*, the carpenter's son was committed to being the provision for our redemption . . . and since right standing with God is manifested through the faithfulness of God combined with our faith in Jesus Christ, we have peace with God . . . awareness of the gift of grace when our faith is exercised.

If we endure life's daily doses of pain and yet believe in the all-sufficient grace of our Lord Jesus Christ. Though tested, life's storms will not consume us. Though raging winds buffet us, in an indiscriminate manner, we ask, as his disciples did in Mark 4:38, "Master, do you not care that we are perishing?" He will respond to you as he did to them: "Why are you afraid when I am in the boat with you? Have you still no faith? Do you not realize that even the wind and the sea obey me?"

The Ministry of Hope

Presumably delivered by the hand of deacon Phoebe, a woman in ministry . . . a servant for sure, but one I'd like to think had some official ecclesiastical status . . . Paul's correspondence to the Roman church is emblematic of what it means to "hope against hope." By all accounts, the apostle thought that by 58 C.E. his work in the churches he had established in the Aegean region had reached fulfillment . . . and all that remained for him to do was to return to the Jerusalem council to empty his collection plate of funds he received from the churches.

This letter, arguably his last, spoke of a veteran's witness about a God who sustains, delivers, and renews those who have put their trust and hope in Jesus. The letter alone testifies of Paul's ministry of hope. Paul was on his way to Spain to embark on a new mission.

When it was beyond hope, Abraham had faith in the hope he would become father of many nations.[24] The text declares that he was fully convinced that God was able to do what God promised. Beyond hope. You know better than I situations that are seemingly beyond hope. You need not go far to see the lamentable crises afflicting the health of African America . . . high incarceration rates, father absenteeism, unwed and teenage pregnancy, domestic abuse and violence, high rates of sexually transmitted diseases, high foreclosure rates, homelessness, joblessness, job discrimination, unaffordable health care, unscrupulous pay-day lending practices targeting the Black working poor, the growing digital information gap . . . diabetes, hypertension, prostate and breast cancer. You need not go far.

When things are seemingly beyond hope, there is the validation that doing ministry is a must. Well, I don't know if I'm called? Get over yourself.

The unambiguous Paul is clear about his belief that Jesus Christ provides both the definitive and most decisive solution to humanity's plight. But he does so with theological tact. He defends his confession but is not defensive. He does not feel threatened in the least by the religious feuding in the Greco-Roman public square. Burning the Koran in a desperate attempt to preserve the Christian ideal would have been thought utterly ridiculous to the apostle Paul . . . grossly antithetical to his theological impulse. I say to you, as Christians in this society of growing religious pluralism, take an assertive posture; defend your confession but don't be defensive.

For Paul, it is clear, the power of sin has been overcome by Jesus' death and resurrection. Paul takes an assertive posture about an eschatological event that has already begun, though not fully complete. We have choices here—that is what postmodernity offers. We can be indifferent, defensive, even obnoxious. Or we can be assertive and respectful about our confessions. It is possible to be a humble, nonthreatened Christian in a postmodern world.

But ownership of this reality is always tensive. In other words, if our Christian confession is authentically built on Christian hope then we have to see ourselves as people on a pilgrimage moving toward an *already, but not yet* unsettling future.

In that now-classic text, *We Have This Ministry*, co-authored by Gardner Taylor and Sam Proctor, Taylor quotes that esteemed Harvard preacher George Buttrick, saying that the Christian minister today has no choice but to rely on a "reverent agnosticism." That is to say, alongside his or her Christly confession ought also be the confession that we are lacking in knowledge about many things about God . . . that we "see through a glass darkly," that there are blind spots yet to be overcome.[25] We know, but we don't know.

You are pinned today, joining an elite vanguard of Howardites, but for this privilege you *should not* boast. Paul says to the church in Rome that our boast should be God-reliant boasting, that we should boast in our hope, not in our intellectual privileges, not in our Ciceronian sophistry or Aristotelian logic. Sister Jones who can't buy her prescription meds don't care nothing about that. Brother Smith who is upside down in his mortgage don't care nothing about that. But boast in our hope of sharing the glory of God. I am persuaded by this hope. There is a ministry of hope that I cling to . . . all hope is, is God's way of liberating us from the shackles of our previous performances, creating in us and around us a new tomorrow, new opportunity, or another chance when there is no evidence that it could be possible.[26]

If we can confidently say in faith and live in such a way that communicates to others that "God is able" to see us through, that alongside God's self we are permitted to participate in what God is doing in the world, then we will have shareholder status. No longer slaves to suffering but shareholders of God's glory.

Be ministers! Have a ministry that matters . . . a ministry worth something. Make no mistake, a faithful ministry engenders pain but it also bestows a gracious privilege . . . the privilege to hope. Welcome to the school of the prophets!

Trivocal Preaching in African America

*Preachers have an awesome task. We dare to stand before
people very much mindful of our weaknesses . . . yet in the midst of
our ever-evolving and becoming selves, we are charged with the
responsibility of proclaiming the everlasting and immutable gospel
of the Lord Jesus Christ. What a responsibility!*

—Charles E. Booth[1]

It is virtually impossible to come to a consensus about what constitutes effective preaching in African American ecclesial contexts. Some suggest that effective preaching is performance driven, soul stirring, direct, and personal. Others claim that pulpit effectiveness has to do with the preacher's dexterity as an expositor of Scripture. Still others chart effectiveness based on the preacher's ability to translate the gospel in culturally relevant modes to fit the times. What can be stated without fear of contradiction is that the gospel is inherently effective. The preacher can make no claims to inherent effectiveness; true effectiveness is doing something with the anointing that blesses and ordains the preacher's work. Effective preachers hear the voice of God calling them into authentic expression to give clear interpretation of Jesus' healing vision of proclaiming release for the captives, recovery of sight to the blind, and emancipation for the oppressed ones.

Trivocal preaching in African America is Christian proclamation. It is speaking words of justice, recovery, and hope. It is the proclamatory ministry of reminding the church community about its present situation and what it must now do to address the crises afflicting the health of Black life in America. I have argued for the recovery of the voice of the African American preacher. A recovered voice under the Spirit's power makes preaching efficacious and meaning making. The preacher's refashioned identity by means of implementing the trivocal impulse in her or his preaching life is not preoccupation with regard to mastering some homiletical technique. Growing in the preaching life is about recovering one's authentic preaching voice in light of what God intends and expects of the preacher as participant in the African American community's restoration project. It has been my contention throughout this book that trivocal preaching—preaching from the three voices of prophet, priest, and sage—is the single most important task in the revitalization of African American churches and communities. More than an emblem of African American worship practice, trivocal preaching is African America's theorhetorical currency for staving off communal death.

Anointed Trivocal Preachers: King, Hall, and Taylor

Martin Luther King Jr.'s preaching erected a social vision for the creation of what he called the "Beloved Community," where people of all races, ethnicities, and class would work together in love and cooperation. King challenged the status quo and, with a commanding baritone, elevated the hopes of Black sufferers in a separate but unequal society. As eulogist at the funeral of the "four little girls" in the Birmingham church bombing, the grief-stricken King's priestly concern ministered to a community in mourning. King's apocalyptic vision ushered in an important ecclesiological shift in America's religious landscape. In march after march, he inspired the masses to preach the gospel with their own feet.

King is quoted as saying, "Prathia Hall is the one platform speaker I would prefer not to follow." American society has made a tremendous blunder in that too great a number do not know the name Prathia Hall. Hall's brilliance as pastor of Mt. Sharon Baptist Church of Philadelphia, preacher of the gospel, and professor of social ethics is only surpassed by her life of advocacy and commitment to the cause of racial and social justice.

Gardner C. Taylor is appropriately lauded as the greatest living Protestant preacher in America today. King idolized Taylor's preaching. Taylor's personal magnetism and poetic genius as a preacher of the gospel has influenced several generations of preachers. "Gardner Calvin Taylor has lived *lives*, not just *a life*." In his collection of milestone moments and memories, Joel C. Gregory so eloquently continues, "He has lived life to the brim, and, like ripened fruit, some of it falls naturally into his creative homiletic art."[2]

These anointed Black preaching trivocalists of the modern era exalted Jesus' vision in their preaching. In spoken word each confronted myriad contradictions of Black life. They routinely conveyed an outlook of divine purpose in their sermons by (1) naming the idolatrous practices and abuses of power in church and societal sin; (2) seeking the care and restoration of souls through Christ's redeeming and reconciling work of comfort; and (3) announcing the providential promises for future generations as fulfilled. Their anointed preaching sought to empower listeners to maintain their dignity and humanity. Consistently forging an alignment with Jesus' inaugural vision, their homiletic visions are instructive for contemporary ministers. Somewhere along their journeys they each found their authentic preaching voice—one that speaks words of justice, recovery, and hope, telling again the church about its present situation and where it must now go.

Martin Luther King Jr.

Excerpts from sermon "I've Been to the Mountaintop."[3] *At Mason Temple Church of God in Christ, in Memphis, Tennessee, the denominational headquarters of the COGIC, before a charged assembly of supporters for the rights of sanitation workers, King delivered this final sermon. He was assassinated the following day.*

THE PROPHETIC VOICE

"We need all of you. And you know what's beautiful to me, is to see all of these ministers of the Gospel. It's a marvelous picture. Who is it that is supposed to articulate the longings and aspirations of the people more than the preacher? Somehow the preacher must be an Amos, and say, 'Let justice roll down like waters and righteousness like a mighty stream.' Somehow, the preacher must say with Jesus, 'The spirit of the Lord is upon me, because he hath anointed me to deal with the problems of the poor.' "[4]

"Well, I don't know what will happen now. We've got some difficult days ahead. But it doesn't matter with me now. Because I've been to the mountaintop. And I don't mind. Like anybody, I would like to live a long life. Longevity has its place. But I'm not concerned about that now. I just want to do God's will. And He's allowed me to go up to the mountain. And I've looked over. And I've seen the promised land. I may not get there with you. But I want you to know tonight, that we, as a people, will get to the promised land."[5]

THE PRIESTLY VOICE

"We are determined to be people. We are saying that we are God's children. And that we don't have to live like we are forced to live. Now, what does all of this mean in this great period of history? It means that we've got to stay together. We've got to stay together and maintain unity."[6]

"When the slaves get together, that's the beginning of getting out of slavery. Now let us maintain unity. Secondly, let us keep the issues where they are. The issue is injustice. The issue is the refusal of Memphis to be fair and honest in its dealings with its public servants, who happen to be sanitation workers."[7]

THE SAGELY VOICE

"Now we're going to march again, and we've got to march again, in order to put the issue where it is supposed to be. And force everybody to see that there are thirteen hundred of God's children here suffering, sometimes going hungry, going through dark and dreary nights wondering how this thing is going to come out. That's the issue."[8]

"That couldn't stop us. And we just went on before the dogs and we would look at them; and we'd go on before the water hoses and we would look at it, and we'd just go on singing 'Over my head I see freedom in the air.' "[9]

"All we say to America is, 'Be true to what you said on paper.' "[10]

Prathia Hall

Excerpts from the sermon "Between the Wilderness and the Cliff,"[11] based on Luke 4:14-15, 20, 28-30: *Then Jesus, filled with the power of the Spirit, returned to Galilee, and a report about him spread through all the surrounding country. He began to teach in their synagogues and was praised by everyone. . . . The eyes of all in the synagogue were fixed on him. Then he began to say to them, "Today this Scripture has been fulfilled in your hearing.". . . When they heard this, all in the synagogue were filled with rage. They got up, drove him out of the town, and led him to the brow of the hill on which their town was built, so that they might hurl him off the cliff. But he passed through the midst of them and went on his way.*

THE PROPHETIC VOICE

"Preacher, if you are really God's anointed woman, just let me name you, let me form you, let me get you to dance to my tune, let me get you to jump at my command, let me get you to do my tricks. Preaching woman, let me tell you who you are, where you belong, when and where you can preach. You can make a pretty good reputation just doing Woman's days. You'll be all right. Just stay in a woman's place."

"My sisters and brothers, a surrendered identity is deadly. It is more deadly than lost identity. Surrendered identity means that you intentionally relinquish who you are, and you voluntarily sell out God's divine ministry."

"How many of us have been seduced by the temptation to prove who we are? But Jesus, our blessed Lord, overcame it. He looked Satan in the face: 'Don't you quote the Word to me. I am the living Word, and I know what I am about.' "[12]

THE PRIESTLY VOICE

"So preachers, teachers, servants of God, don't you get tangled up between the wilderness and the cliff. Don't you surrender your identity. Sister preacher, whether they believe you or not, you [sic] better know who you are."

"The God who has called us is the God who has consecrated us, is the God who is right now, right now anointing us."[13]

THE SAGELY VOICE

"My friends, the context of our ministries is between the wilderness and the cliff, but we are able to escape the crowd. He escaped through their midst. We escape the people, but only through the very people who would hurl us over the cliff, for these are the people whom God has called us to serve. These are the people whom God will save through our ministries. The temptation at the cliff is contempt for the crowd. But don't you surrender to contempt. Your escape is not in their hands."

"The path of ministry is through the midst of the people. It's in the ministry to which we are called and for which we have been consecrated. So wherever the people are, that's the preaching place, the teaching place, and we have just one sermon: Good news to the poor, deliverance to the captives, sight to the blind, healing for the broken, and freedom for the oppressed."[14]

Gardner C. Taylor

Excerpts from the sermon "Parting Words."[15] *Based on Revelation 22:18-19, and companion texts Matthew 5:5; Isaiah 61:3; 40:31; and 43:2, this was Taylor's final sermon as pastor of Concord Baptist Church, Brooklyn, New York, June 24, 1990.*

THE PROPHETIC VOICE

"God's Word does not need to be added to. I look back on my responsibility as a preacher called of God and ask myself if ever I tried to make the Word of God mean what I wanted it to mean. I pray not. Our guidebook is not a partial report. Human documents need amendment and adjustment. The original Constitution of the United States identified you and me as three-fifths of a citizen. That needed to be changed, and the cost in blood and money and human anguish is still being paid. The coming of our distinguished visitor from South Africa this week has reminded us that people can write the loftiest language and hide in it deadly poison and the ugliest oppression. Nelson Mandela said that there is a whole body of law in South Africa which must be changed."[16]

THE PRIESTLY VOICE

"I leave to all who long to know God better the precious promise of his: 'Blessed are they which hunger and thirst after righteousness: for they shall be filled' (Matt. 5:5). The grace of the Lord Jesus Christ be with you all. I leave to any who are sad the ancient promise that God will 'give the garment of praise for the spirit of heaviness' (Isa. 61:3). The grace of our Lord Jesus Christ be with you all. I leave to all who feel weary on the way the word from on high, 'They that wait upon the Lord shall renew their strength' (Isa. 40:31). The grace of the Lord Jesus Christ be with you all. I leave to all who with me grow old and feel the mist of Jordan spraying on wrinkled brows, 'When thou passest through the waters, I will be with thee' (Isa. 43:2). The grace of our Lord Jesus Christ be with you all."[17]

THE SAGELY VOICE

"What does one say at the last when there is so much left to be said? Here or wherever young men and women of ministry may hear about this hour, I will pass on to them a legacy which is a promise. Have no anxiety about what you will preach to the people Sunday after Sunday, year after year, decade after decade."[18]

"The last words of the Bible are an earnest wish and a fervent prayer, and I give them now to you in parting. The Bible starts with 'In the beginning, God.' It ends appropriately with 'The grace of our Lord Jesus Christ be with you all.' It was what John left as his great vision ended, a kind of last will and testament.

"And so, my people, I have little of this world's honor or goods to give you now at evening. As I surrender this command, I do not have a highly acclaimed position to leave to you. As I take my departure and go out of this pulpit for the last time as pastor, I cannot leave to you pride of place, nor do I have the applause of the world to give you as my legacy.

"I do offer something by God's grace. I leave to my successor, the Reverend Gary Simpson, the promise of his Savior, 'I will be with you.'

And may our pastor know a long, bright joy here. The grace of the Lord Jesus Christ be with him."[19]

"A Symphony of Voices": Other Sermon Excerpts

Having discussed the trivocal impulse in King, Hall, and Taylor's anointed preaching, we turn now in this section to selected sermon excerpts from a diverse cadre of contemporary African American clerics. While I make no claim that the preachers featured here consistently or in reality adhere to or have answered the trivocal beckoning I have commended in this work, what follows are sermon fragments that I think conspicuously illustrate some specific dimension(s) of the prophetic, priestly, or sagely voices of Christian preaching.

Prophetic Soundings

JAMES A. FORBES JR.

One notices in a sermon delivered by the Reverend Dr. James A. Forbes Jr., formerly Senior Minister of The Riverside Church, New York City, that there is a practical side to the prophetic message.[20] In a sermon preached at Rockefeller Memorial Chapel at the University of Chicago on November 9, 2003, Forbes speaks to the aftermath of 9/11. His sermon focuses on Amos 7, where God promises God's people a plumb line (a standard by which one can measure if things are in line) in the midst of their trouble. Guided by the distinctive elements of the paradigm, he declares:

> Now, let me say for those of us who are in New York, we are in the process now of getting ready to reconstruct the World Trade Center and, ideologically and metaphorically, we really need to make sure that we have a plumb line by which we are building. Everybody now knows that we cannot afford faulty construction. We need to know that whatever we are building, not only in terms of real estate, but in terms of the values of our nation that they will not depart from the blue print as reflected in the Constitution or the Bill of Rights. . . . How dare we build our nation or attempt to rebuild other nations unless the plumb line of justice and compassion and equality and ecological sensibility is hanging straight so that we do not deviate,

for it could be perilous not only for us, but for the nations we will be able to influence.[21]

DEFOREST BLAKE SOARIES JR.

Based on the parable of the fig tree told by Jesus to his disciples in Luke 13:6-8, in a sermon titled, "Bear Some Fruit," Soaries, the former New Jersey Secretary of State, forcefully declares to his several-thousand-member, affluent African American congregation that God holds disdain for church ministries that cherish their prestige, physical, and material well-being while the community surrounding its doors languishes and the church seems increasingly less committed to its Lord and mission. In this sermon, the barren fig tree represents both Christian individuals and African American churches themselves that have lost their way and have become confused about its mission to the world in service to Jesus Christ.

> This fig tree forgot that its only purpose was to produce figs. . . . Jesus said in John chapter 15 that if you are going to be my disciples you've got to bear some fruit. He didn't say you've got to join the usher board, to write big checks. Jesus says, "If you are going to be my disciple you've got to be a fruit bearer . . . look at how many houses have been built by Episcopalians, look at what Presbyterians have done, look at what Baptist mission has done." God did not plant us in this vineyard so that we could just "be."

Using the same controlling image, Soaries shifts his analysis to further discuss a fig tree's influence on other fig trees:

> Did you know that when this fig tree failed to produce fruit it was a threat to other fig trees? You see, once you see one tree with no fruit it creates in your mind that if this tree is barren then the next tree might be barren and it can cause somebody to give up on fig trees.[22]

JEREMIAH WRIGHT JR.

In the excerpt that follows, Rev. Dr. Wright's criticism is directed at perceived shortcomings of both church and state.[23] His sermon title alone, "Reclaiming Prophetic Ministry: It's Hard Out Here for a Prophet," from

Mark 1:1-4, reveals a connection with the culture and signals his homiletical intent. Suspicious of the government's domesticating influence in suppressing the Black preacher's cry for justice, the preacher Wright denounces in this sermon Black clergy's double-dealing and self-serving behaviors with established power. A master of poetic adornment, he juxtaposes John the Baptist's prophetic ministry with today's preachers of "health-and-wealth." Wright exclaims:

> Today's prosperity preachers count as their claim to fame that they have access to the White House. As Esau sold his birthright for a mess of pottage these folks have sold their souls and their people out for a mess of money. Hush mouth benefits or tax cuts from the President and you get them free and with lockjaw. They can't open their mouths to speak the truth in the presence of such high-profile liars . . . they are lying about weapons of mass destruction. They see no evil with rapes in Baghdad . . . spying on millions of Americans. They hear no evil when about forty-six million people are without health care. They see no evil and hear no evil . . . look at the victims of Katrina. They see no evil . . . our megachurch ministers hear no truth because the . . . dog can't howl when he's got a bone in his mouth. They have access to the White House but have lockjaw in the process.[24]

But, not long after this scathing rebuke, what is revealed in Wright's preaching is his own commitment to be prophetic, that is, to reject flatly the status quo and to energize persons and communities by the promise of a new future that God intends.[25] He expresses,

> Mark writes: a lone voice crying out in the wilderness preaching the baptism of repentance, and the forgiveness of sins . . . it is that proclamation which is the final reason it is hard out here for a prophet . . . because of what we have to preach. Proclamation leads one into the process of transformation . . . restoration, wholeness for God's purposes.[26]

J. ALFRED SMITH JR.

Jeremiah 26:1-2 is the textual ground upon which this sermon is based.[27] The message is instructive for ministers, the church, and the academy. Jeremiah's oracle to King Jehoiakim, son of Josiah of Judah, that is presented in this text comes with a directive for the king to give a courageous message to all the cities of Judah. Smith exposits the text and our contemporary situation, paying attention to the manifold ills that continue to cripple African American communities. He articulates the abusive practices of clergy and offers a strong critique of prosperity theology and the nation's public-policy agenda. Smith levels this critique of false speaking in ministry practice:

> False prophetic speech is lying speech. False priestly ministry abuses authority—but the people love it that way. False prophetic speech is popular, partisan, patriotic, and pleasing to priest, prophet, and people. False priestly ministry is governed by the self-interests of maintaining institutional survival at all costs; but the God-called prophet proclaims, 'Thus saith the Lord' at any price. How sad that professional malpractice of priests and prophets becomes status quo religious practice that the people love.[28]

Imagining what the prophet Jeremiah would say to the social crisis of America's cities in a social environment where ministers fall into the trappings of materialism, Smith inquires,

> Would Jeremiah be as welcome in today's cities as megachurch television preachers who fly in privately owned jets to preach to full-capacity audiences in the coliseums where professional athletes perform? Would Jeremiah be welcome in today's cities if he preached the arrogance of greed, the immoral use of brutalizing power on the poor and the powerless? Would Jeremiah be welcome in today's cities to talk about a freedom of speech that promotes unholy speech? Would groups that promote abortion in today's cities applaud Jeremiah for saying that God formed him in his mother's womb?[29]

Though Smith's criticism is strident, he clearly sees that criticism in the absence of hope is of no use to his hearers. In this case, he points out that Jeremiah's oracle indicts the people for their sins but God offers the same people inspiration and hope for redemption. He says,

> Jeremiah soon learned what our elders learned. He learned that there is a balm in Gilead. Sometimes, we may feel discouraged. We may think our work is in vain, but then the Holy Spirit revives our souls again; there is a balm in Gilead . . .

Resurrection comes to pass. Listen to the sounds of joy and gladness. The old is passed away. The new explodes at springtime. Thawing ice turns into running waters from winter's last snow. Birds pierce the air with song. After trees awaken from a long winter's sleep, flowers bud on the branches. But the best is yet to come.

'The days are surely coming, says the LORD, when I will fulfill the promise I made to the house of Israel and the house of Judah. In those days and at that time I will cause a righteous Branch to spring up for David; and he shall execute justice and righteousness in the land.' [Jer. 33:14-15][30]

Finally, he challenges and exhorts preachers,

Prophetic preachers of the twenty-first century, speak to the cities; speak to America about this branch. Speak about this branch or root who emerged out of dry ground until America the ugly becomes America the beautiful. Lift up your voice, prophetic preachers, so that ears deafened by sin will hear clearly good news for a bad news world. . . . Stand on your tiptoes and speak and gaze into the future until you can see the majestic coming of the Lord, as King of kings and Lord of lords.[31]

Priestly Listening

WAYNE E. CROFT SR.

In this sermon, entitled "A Candidate for the Hall of Faith," based on Genesis 28:8 ("Then Abraham breathed his last and died at a good old age, an old man and full of years; and he was gathered to his people"), Pastor Croft preaches the funeral sermon of his father, Deacon Rice Croft.[32] On a few occasions pastors are called to the difficult task of eulogizing their close of kin. In many traditions, assuming such a task is normally advised against, for a number of reasons. But it is clear, from this deeply reflective sermon, that no one could have painted a better family portrait of father and son than this son has about his father. Croft begins the sermon this way:

One of my dad's favorite sports was professional baseball. He would watch baseball day in and day out. As a young boy, I remember watching baseball games with him, not because I liked them, but I knew how much he loved the game. One of the unique things the National Baseball League does is it honors its elite players and coaches by placing those both living and dead in the Hall of Fame. . . . In Cooperstown, New York, you will find the names, pictures, and jerseys of their great players. Players like William Julius "Judy" Johnson, the first African American to be elected to the NBL Hall of Fame, Jackie Robinson, and Hank Aaron.

Although there is no Hall of Fame in the Bible, there is located in Hebrews 11 what I like to refer to as the Hall of Faith. In this Hall of Faith are the names of great men and women such as Abel, Enoch, Noah, Sarah, Isaac . . . and of course, Abraham, the father of the faithful.

If God, however, looked favorably upon me as God did the Hebrew writer, gave me a pen and a piece of paper, and told me to write a postmodern list of those would should be elected to the Hall of Faith, the first name I would list without reservation is Rice Croft.[33]

NOEL JONES

Pastor Jones takes his text from Romans 8:26-31.[34] The focus of his message is on the Holy Spirit's power to sustain the life of believers. Jones offers in this sermon words of consolation to those in distressing situations, shouldering heavy burdens in their daily lives. The following excerpts, taken from a rather lengthy discourse and that appear to have been delivered extemporaneously, highlight the preacher's emphasis on why believers should anticipate help from a God who has been journeying with them all along. In the next lines, Jones urges his listeners to move through their crisis moments with an expectation that God helps:

> I know to pray that God saves me. I know to pray that God will make a way. But now in the middle of a crisis I need a right-now, just-for-this-moment prayer. I needed a right-now prayer a while ago in the middle of a crisis.[35]
>
> When Paul speaks of *help*, it's action of a person coming to another's aid by taking hold of the person or helping to carry the load. The person helping does not take the entire load, but the person helps the individual who is in the crisis. In other words, God is

not going to move me from my fears and from a little nervousness and a little caution. He's not going to take my cognitive energy and put it at bay. No, I'm going to feel it. I'm going to think about it. I'm going to be exercised in the fears and the faith. I'm going to be caught between anxiety and rest. I'm going to be caught between he will or he won't. I'm going to be caught between the greater is he that's in me than the greater that's in the world.[36]

So, even though I am sitting here facing reality, I still have expectation and I still have present help in the power of the Holy Ghost. It's that help that kept me from losing my mind . . . from making the wrong move . . . from being desperate and making a fool out of myself over something I need to wait for God to bring.[37]

GENNIFER BROOKS

Dr. Brooks's sermon, "A Matter of Choice," holds two texts (2 Kings 5:14—story of Naaman; Mark 1:40—story of the unnamed leper) in tension as the sermon's plot line unfolds.[38] This sermon is about the twin powers—pride and humility—and their effects on our life perspective and service to God. Brooks discusses in detail the indiscriminate nature of falling victim to a health crisis (in this story it is leprosy), and how suffering and affliction can paralyze one's outlook on life and potentially thwart the believer from gaining his or her needed access to the healing power found in Jesus Christ. Ironically, like more than a few sermons preached from (Old) First Testament passages by African Americans, she, unsurprisingly, though creatively, ends the sermon with a christocentric turn. Put differently, in this sermon, Hebrew Scripture is interpreted in light of the message of the gospel of Jesus Christ. Consider the following excerpt, where she listens for the priestly voice and addresses the issue of pride:

> Pride causes us to do and say and be what we do not want. Pride causes us to act contrary to God's law, to live contrary to God's plan of salvation for us. Pride pushes us into a cycle of disobedience, sin, sorrow, loss, and pain. It's a matter of choice.
>
> While it took others to help Naaman understand that the choice for a new life was in his hands, the leper understood for himself that this was his only choice for getting a new life. The unnamed leper, who had already lost whatever place he once had in society, knew

that reaching out to Jesus was all that he could do. And he did it.
"[Lord], if you choose, you can make me clean."
"I do choose. Be made clean."[39]

BRAD R. BRAXTON

Phillipians 4:6-7 offers sound guidance to anxious Christians in a dizzy-paced postmodern culture. It reads: "Do not worry about anything, but in everything by prayer and supplication with thanksgiving let your requests be made known to God. And the peace of God, which surpasses all understanding, will guard your hearts and your minds in Christ Jesus."

In his sermon "Hanging Loose in an Uptight World," Braxton takes the listening congregation on a ride that, oddly, from its outset, is anxiety raising and unsettling.[40] Put differently, Braxton, to use Eugene Lowry's language for sermon plot development, "upsets the equilibrium." He opens this way,

> There is a killer on the loose. Law enforcement agencies have never succeeded in tracking this killer down. Having never been arrested or indicted, this killer has no "rap sheet" and has never served a day in prison. This killer, nonetheless, has aided and abetted in the deaths of countless people . . .[41]

Then, following this very brief opening, he provides his listeners a clue about this killer—its nature and patterns—without "telling too much, too soon," to borrow Fred Craddock's preacherly caution.

> We all need to be very aware because this killer might have targeted one of us.
>
> As I have described this killer, I am not sure what face or name has come to your mind. The killer I have in mind is *stress*. Do not fool yourself. Stress can be lethal! Recently, some psychiatrists have coined a term, toxic worry. This term—toxic worry—suggests that stress can set in motion physiological and psychological processes that might contribute directly or indirectly to our dysfunction and destruction.[42]

After illustrating stress causers in a "post–9/11 world," he consults Paul's letter first addressed to the Philippians. For a life filled with toxic worry, he prescribes the following antidote:

Prayer is the prescription. Prayer is the key. Prayer is the answer. In verse 6, there is a marvelous parallelism. In the first clause, Paul says, "Worry about nothing." He begins the second clause by exclaiming, "but in everything with prayer." Did you catch it? Worry about *no* thing. Pray about *every* thing.[43]

To hang loose, pray frequently and pray fervently.[44]

Sagely Rehearsal

VIOLET L. FISHER

Bishop Fisher's sermon bespeaks of a preacher who has traveled widely; one committed to the work of missions and evangelism and social action.[45] In her sermon "Bread for the Journey," she pairs Isaiah 55:1-3 with John 6:25-35, and, thematically, addresses our need to have our hunger satiated by physical (bread) and spiritual (Bread). The sermon does not dichotomize physical and spiritual needs, for both, argues Fisher, are essential forms of nourishment. Rather, what she ably does is hold both passages in creative tension. Again, like Brooks's sermon, the Old (First) Testament is interpreted in light of how the New (Second) Testament gives witness to Jesus Christ.

The literary form of the Isaiah 55 text itself presents the preacher an ideal set-up for sermonizing. The prophet raises a basic question that invites a thoughtful response: Why spend money on what is not bread, and your labor on what does not satisfy? (v. 2).

Before interpreting both Scripture passages and discussing their application, and eschewing esoteric nonsense, Fisher begins her sermon by making very mundane, practical, descriptive claims, using the loaded term *bread* as a controlling image and metaphoric construct.

> "Bread" is a good word. "Bread" is a word we use often around our homes. Bread is so important to life. I'm sure most of you have a memo pad with a pen or pencil near your refrigerator where the list for groceries is compiled as you run out of things. I am sure that at the top of every list, in every household is the word "Bread," the universal food for our bodies. . . . I have been fortunate enough to visit and experience many different breads: Italian, New York rye, Matzo crackers, whole wheat bread, English muffins, bagels,

shortbread, scones, Greek pastries, white bread, and my favorite, cornbread.[46]

Jesus knew the needs of the human body. Remember, he hungered and thirsted in the wilderness. He grew up in a Jewish home where his mother, Mary, as part of her daily routine and responsibilities made bread. Jesus used bread in the Passover meal. He fed 5,000 people with five loaves of bread because he had compassion on them. He would not permit them to go home hungry. In a family, the one who brings home the most money is called, "the bread-winner." When we take a job we ask ourselves a question, "Can I put bread on the table for my family?" The word "bread" has so many meanings and emotions attached to it.[47]

Later on in the sermon, she makes the Christo-/theocentric turn:

Sisters and brothers, our Bread is God himself and God gives himself to us as food. Jesus provides more than a meal. Jesus provides a moment in which we can give ourselves to God. . . . Yes, there is a need for bread that keeps us alive. There is also a need for bread that gives us a reason to live.[48]

HAYWOOD A. ROBINSON III

In a sermon titled "Standing Resolutions," delivered on the first Communion Sunday of 2010, Robinson calls the church officers and ministry leaders serving the People's Community Baptist Church in Silver Spring, Maryland, to a renewed commitment in fulfilling their various ministry objectives. Based on Joshua 4:16, where Joshua gathers the tribes and commands them to set stones of remembrance to remind them of God's faithful work in their journeying as a chosen people, Robinson's fivefold message outlines for contemporary Christians what it means to make lasting resolutions as God-fearers.

Give God a standing resolution that you will forsake the wrong gods. Fear the Lord and put away false gods in the land of Egypt . . . in America money has become God . . . when these gods compromise us we will bow our knees to them.

This is not like the fitness resolution. You start a gym membership in January and stop in March . . . a standing resolution is something that will last the life of His child. Stones will listen to your commitment and they will be a witness to your commitment to follow His Word.

Bringing the sermon toward a christocentric climax, he reiterates the sermon's focus:

> We've got to do at least five things: forsake other gods; fear the wrath of God; follow the Word of God; fulfill the will of God; and, finish the work of God.
>
> Joshua finished his work. Moses finished his work. David finished his work. Another Yeshua came and finished his work. But what about you and me?[49]

WILLIAM D. WATLEY

In a sermon entitled "Two Roads to the Same Place," from Mark 1:16 and 15:21, Pastor Watley develops two characters, placing them side by side and running their stories in parallel.[50] Both characters share the name: Simon. Both have distinct personalities and divergent backgrounds—one is an intimate companion and disciple of Jesus and the other is an African who encounters Jesus on his way to Calvary's cross. Watley asks his listeners to have a broader theological perspective on what it means to "come to Jesus." He maintains that Jesus accepts all who believe no matter who they are or where they meet him on their journey. As sage he preaches a christocentric message overheard by an obviously intergenerational constituency of listeners. He calls believers to self-examination.

> Sometimes we spend too much time debating with each other about how we became believers or followers of the Lord Jesus Christ. How often have we heard the saints say, "My background is Baptist or Methodist or Catholic or Pentecostal," or, "I've been here for forty years and you just got here?" What difference does it make in the long run what the street is named or how long or short it is, or how long we've been on it, as long as it leads to the right place—the arms of Jesus, the love of Jesus, the forgiveness of Jesus, the peace of Jesus, and the joy of Jesus.[51]

Sagely Rehearsal and Priestly Listening

SAMUEL J. GILBERT SR. AND SAMUEL J. GILBERT II

In its Fall 2002 issue "It's a Family Affair," the editors of the quarterly journal the *African American Pulpit* explored the topic of African American clergy families, specifically, a consideration of varied preaching family models. Featured are sermons of parent and child, husband and wife, and sibling pairs, and some attention is given to extensive lineage dynamics where it appears that preaching flows from one's DNA or some other close-of-kin circumstance.

Due to my obvious bias, having found an extensive, traceable preaching legacy in my family system, here I make no strong judgments about the matter. In this particular issue are sermons by the late Washington Monroe Trotter and son Gardner C. Taylor, the late H. Beecher Hicks Sr. and his son H. Beecher Hicks Jr.; clergy couples such as John R. Bryant and Cecelia Williams Bryant, and Floyd and Elaine Flake; and finally, siblings, such as brothers Melvin and J. C. Wade.[52]

What follows are excerpts from sermons preached by my own relatives, Samuel J. Gilbert Sr. and Samuel J. Gilbert II, respectively, senior pastor emeritus and senior pastor of the Mt. Sinai Baptist Church in Houston, Texas. J. Weldon Gilbert, whose sermon is not featured here, is a younger minister son of S. J. Gilbert Sr. My decision to highlight members of my family could rightly earn me an accusation of preferential treatment, but more than the others listed above, I have had frequent and direct acquaintance with their preaching.

Following the September 11, 2001, tragedy, in his sermon "How to Handle Conflict in the World," S. J. Gilbert Sr. functions as sage when he draws on the familiar passage in Romans 8, which reads: "And we know that in all things God works for the good of those who love him, who have been called according to his purpose." The sermon addresses local and national, personal and communal aspects of crisis realities in American culture. The sermon seeks to persuade the hearers that based on God's demonstrated reliability and active work throughout Scripture they can find great success when faith in God is channeled in the situation of crisis. Gilbert begins:

> Where does conflict come from? One moment your sky of life is
> clear; the next you can be buffeted, beaten, and slapped about by

strong winds and torrential rainstorms. Storms are like that. They often appear out of nowhere at the wrong time and are totally inconvenient. They disrupt our plans and leave devastation in their path. Life is never the same after some storms, battles, collisions, and conflicts have swept through our lives.[53]

Later on, pointing out a path to confront life's conflicts, he says,

You can handle conflict if you realize that God will protect those who love the Lord. . . . We in America are still in a position to see God working things out for us. We must cooperate with God instead of turning our backs on him.[54]

Following a priestly course, S. J. Gilbert II takes on a christological focus, declaring that Christ died for humanity's sins and offers forgiveness—absolution of sin to those with repentant hearts. In his sermon entitled "A Dedication to the Cause of Christ," supported by Acts 5, in his opening words he reminds the churched and unchurched that they cannot escape God's watch nor dealing with self.

Nowadays most people aren't committed. . . . Nowadays nobody is loyal to churches. They're in and out of churches, in and out, going to church here, going to church there. There isn't loyalty anymore.

The fact that there is no loyalty is indicative of the fact that we don't have commitment. And where there's no commitment, there's no dedication. We're not dedicated. I'm trying to say that we give up too easily. We give up on good stuff too quick. That's where dedication comes in. When you're able to endure, you stand. Yeah. You can't run.

Let me share something with you. If you start running, you'll always be running, because there's always something wrong—everywhere you go. Because *you* are everywhere you go. (Y'all will catch that on the way home.) And ain't no need of you trying to get away from yourself. You never get away from you. You know the imperfection lies within you.

And so, in our sermon tonight, we find that these apostles were some dedicated folk. They were committed and dedicated to the task in the midst of adversity. Amen. The only way you can test your dedication is in adversity. Anybody can be dedicated when nothing is happening, you know. But it's when the tough times hit, how dedicated can you be? Do you run off and run away and try to bury your problems? Or do you tough it out?[55]

• • •

In a violent and fragmented culture of fear and death, amid the broad range of complex congregational and community concerns and expectations, preaching remains the most vital task in addressing the mammoth social and ecclesial crises of our times. In the process of drawing on sermons of a representative vanguard of Black clergy, I have identified various marks that are paradigmatic of trivocal preaching as a ministry of Christian proclamation. Moreover, I have maintained that there are constructive tools available for preachers who are willing to reclaim and refashion their ministries from a three-dimensional vantage. I am utterly convinced that only a preaching ministry that takes seriously the prophetic, priestly, and sagely dynamics that flow from a holistic preaching life can be profitable, viable, and a renewing source of healing and strength for at-risk communities and churches. The final chapter moves our focus from hearing trivocal voices of contemporary Black preaching toward a typological exploration of the preacher's social identity, as a key to finding one's own voice.

6

What the Church Expects, What the Village Needs

Who is it that is supposed to articulate the longings and aspirations of the people more than the preacher?

—Martin Luther King Jr.[1]

S elf-understanding is vital to the preacher's preaching life. A minister's preaching life is comprised of much more than sermons and illustrations; it is defined by the preacher's life engagements, personal character, theological impulses, and vocational commitments. But few obtain an appropriate interpretation of the African American preacher's complex self-identity. One inattentive to a congregation's expectations of the preacher and the preacher's social identity and function within a specific religious community will have severely deficient knowledge about why the single most important voice for staving off the death of African American communities is the preacher's.

Who is it that is supposed to articulate the longings and aspirations of the people more than the preacher? The preacher's capacity, as spiritual guide, to gather up the needs and hopes of an awaiting congregation and to interpret them in light of the gospel is essential to the preacher's work. Thus, the preacher's awareness of self as minister is of great importance. Who a minister understands herself or himself to be as preacher of the

Word has major implications for her or his methods of preparation and the practices he or she performs within the community.

Thomas G. Long maintains that "if ministers picture themselves as 'shepherds' or 'prophets' or 'enablers' or 'evangelists' or 'spiritual entrepreneurs' or 'servant leaders' or 'wounded healers,' these guiding images of ministry will prompt them to emphasize certain tasks of ministry and to minimize others. They will speak and act in the ways demanded by those images."[2]

We Wear the Masks: Faces of the Black Preacher

Who are these Black religious leaders that have captured the sacred imagination of the faithful and at the same time have earned worldwide scrutiny? Centuries have passed since the rise of the Black preacher in North America and yet, outside of dreadful caricature, the wider culture remains badly informed about the social identity of and functional roles performed by the Black preacher in our society today. Before providing concluding thoughts about the perceived needs and expectations of congregations of their preachers, in the next segment of this final chapter, I offer a descriptive typology for the reader to think more deeply about the intricate life-world of the contemporary Black preacher.[3]

A preacher's persona or *prosopon*, meaning "face" in Greek, is not simply a mask behind which she or he performs a role in a socioreligious drama. While the term *persona* carries multiple meanings in the culture, for our purposes, "persona" may be defined as one's social identity and function within a specific religious community. A persona is a subsistent role whereby the role and speaker are one. We bring ourselves to the scriptural texts we interpret, and always is the congregation's expectation inseparable from the preacher's social identity.

Let us consider seven African American preacher personas: (1) *Evangelical-Moralist*, (2) *Social Activist*, (3) *Entrepreneurial Agent*, (4) *Clerico-Politician*, (5) *Rancher-Pontiff*, (6) *Mystic-Spiritualist*, and (7) *Social Poet–Technophile*. Before delving into their specifics, however, we need to be clear what this typology is and is not. My goals here are modest in respect to what an evidence-based study would demand. I have two simple aims: first, using such a typology helps to bring into better focus my thesis concerning the need for African American preachers to reconceive their self-identity in a violent, fragmented, postmodern, and increasingly pluralistic age. Second, I hope to provide readers a meaningful, though brief, assessment about each type's constructive features, noting in particular the potential hazards that arise when the *prosopon* of the preacher supplants the *prosopon* of Christ in the ministry of preaching.

My descriptions are metaphoric constructions. Metaphors associate two distinct things; that is, one thing is the representation of another. As with most any literary device involving the use of language, metaphors depart from their literal meaning to create an image or picture in the mind of the reader. To refer to a preacher as an "evangelical-moralist" or "social poet" is to know that these terms are shorthand for a larger reality toward which I have perceived a preacher is tending. Some particular ideological or theological commitment goes hand in hand with each persona. Thus, some overlap in what is classified should be expected, as a preacher will likely identify with more than one persona type. This is why metaphoric constructions are useful. It is highly unlikely that a minister could fulfill his or her duties and obligations to the community if he or she is circumscribed to one persona type. Still, what I am suggesting is that every African American preacher will lean toward one type more than another. Perhaps the most important feature of this typology is that it provides some angle of vision into the highly differentiated, complex character of the African American preacher.

Evangelical-Moralist

The Evangelical-Moralist (E-M) takes seriously the message of Christianity as recorded in the Bible, holding fast to the hermeneutic that God speaks and is revealed through Scripture. Accordingly, an E-M places strong emphasis on the believer's need for a personal relationship with Jesus Christ through spiritual conversion, baptism, and soul regeneration. It is also the believer's obligation to be an active witness in response to his or her redeemed status to the end of soul winning or spreading the gospel message by teaching, evangelism, and preaching.

The experienced Evangelical-Moralist is skillful in apologetics as well as teaching Christian doctrine; he or she has encyclopedic ability to reference, quote, and use Scripture for ministry practice. This preacher tends to catalog problems and focuses on his or her hearer's life concerns, instructing them to embrace specific values and abide by certain norms that should be carried out in one's personal decision making, spiritual devotion, conduct at home, work, and the church.

The strength of the Evangelical-Moralist's preaching is that he or she is able to draw on the major themes and narratives of Christian Scripture and from them offer instructions for individuals in need of spiritual, moral, and ethical direction to apply to their lives. However, with an E-M's compulsive need for every sermon to be prescriptive, clear-cut, and propositional, in his or her preaching there is always the danger of reducing the text to fit problem-solution schemes, to make points and subpoints, or to support the preacher's mnemonic techniques. E-Ms run the high risk of delivering a steady diet of rigid dogmatic principles rather than sermons. For this reason, it is, of course, also likely that their sermons will leave hearers no room for questions and thus diminish any acknowledgment of God's mysterious nature and work.

Social Activist

The Social Activist (SA) maintains that human beings are capable of carrying out ethical action and, directly or indirectly, effecting social change. On policy matters, community concerns, and humanitarian causes, the SA insists on the release of various goods and services to be used for community empowerment and giving assistance to those individuals on the margins of society. For the SA the content-function of the gospel's message is primarily sociopolitical.

Social Activists criticize liturgical practices and the application of the Scriptures that do not prepare or prompt believers to actively engage larger community concerns (e.g., racial profiling, homelessness, poverty, gender discrimination, rape, domestic abuse, etc.). With skills to organize individuals at the local grassroots level and to generate concern around a particular issue or incident, the experienced SA garners wide support from the congregation and, in some cases, earns the "radical reverend" label. The SA's sermons tend to be thematic and topical instead of following an expository pattern. Instead of the sermon perhaps ending in celebration in the spirit of the folk tradition, hearers are left burdened by a challenge or a call to action, often to fulfill some unsettling assignment.

The great strength of the Social Activist's sermon is the consistent message that it broadcasts. That message simply states that Christians have a greater obligation than other persons of goodwill to develop a social consciousness around the work of alleviating of human suffering, rebuilding lives of the marginalized, and challenging the systems that endorse oppressive acts. The SA preacher is always in danger of proof texting. Rather than preaching the whole counsel of Scripture, SAs might easily be drawn to preach public policy to support a political or secular agenda under the guise of preaching the gospel's concern for social welfare and political justice. And when Scripture is consulted, SAs may over privilege the prophetic literature and Jesus' teachings for preaching to the disregard of other valuable texts. Of course, a SA preacher is of little use without some righteous indignation in the bones. But with righteous anger SAs often need to be reminded to be disciplined in their anger and to recognize, above all, that the essence of the gospel is love and its fruits as described in Galatians 4:22-24.

Entrepreneurial Agent

The Entrepreneurial Agent (EA) is a positive thinker and team motivator who uses Scripture in various ways to educate her or his congregation to organize, manage, administrate, and oversee enterprising ventures for the congregation. EAs follow in the spirit of Old Testament exemplars such as Abraham, Joseph, and Jacob, persons recorded as having great wealth and divine favor. The EA takes initiative to build social and financial networks and to increase the power and exposure of their particular congregation.

The Entrepreneurial Agent clearly recognizes that the religious leader must combine keen intellect with good public-relations skills to build financial and social capital for his or her congregation. To put into place various initiatives and projects, preachers of this mold are, in effect, brokers on behalf of the congregation toward expanding the capabilities of the group. A pragmatist interested in outcomes and assessments, the EA's practical concern with market-research statistics, financial-giving predictions, and attendance levels may foster congregational trust or give the impression that the congregation's leadership is principally concerned with church growth and ministry receipts.

In areas of finance, employment, and education, the Entrepreneurial Agent preaches sermons to empower listeners to overcome a victim mind-set. However, because the EA generally focuses on the bottom line, she or he may unwittingly undermine her or his more important charge to provide hospitality and congregational care for believers of all walks of life. The EA's sermons are generally clear-cut and unambiguous; they are sermons with a telos—having a clear end or candid projection into the future. It would not be unusual to see an EA preach from PowerPoint slides or make use of the latest social-networking technologies to increase intimacy with her or his membership. Again, preaching as an EA becomes detrimental to the community's health when services are viewed as trans-actions and persons are treated as commodities.

Clerico-Politician

The Clerico-Politician (C-P) intertwines ecclesiastical headship with civic involvement. Thus, this preacher is typically orally versatile and skilled in the art and science of politics. He or she may be an elected official, an aspirant, or neither. The primary clerical role of the C-P is to be the congregation's chief spokesperson and informant. To expand an old adage, the C-P preaches with the Bible in one hand and a newspaper in the other, or, more contemporarily speaking, simply from an all-in-one digital cell-phone device. The C-P researches political trends and offers political insights on where the community must stand in order to engage effectively the intense moral and social crises of the times.

Like the Social Activist, one of the great strengths of the Clerico-Politician is his or her conviction that Christians should speak in the public square and exercise influence in secular society. The congregation entrusts the C-P to serve their best interests through legislative processes, lobbying, political antagonism, and creating governmental and fiduciary alliances deemed advantageous for the common good, but specifically for those community constituents whom the preacher has been elected or called to serve. They are influential advocates for issues such as voting rights, educational reform, housing discrimination, and employment.

Clerico-Politicians make use of a variety of sermonic approaches depending on the needs of the day. Even still, because C-Ps tend to be busy reverends dividing their time between church and civic affairs, they tend to be highly pragmatic in their methods of sermon preparation. One com-mon approach is for them to carve out space to devote a set block of study time to prepare a sermon series to be preached over an extended period on a selected topic. More often than not the C-P's sermons are the preacher's choice, following no particular planning methodology. These sermons are also usually quasi-expository or topical in nature, and the community's corporate concerns tend to guide the preacher's hermeneutic.

The major shortcoming of the Clerico-Politician involves his or her proclivities to blur the lines of church-state relations, or to allow partisan politics or quest for greater influence and power to overshadow his or her ministerial charge to be the community's priest. In addition to being community spokesperson, C-Ps have to work hard to be a congregation's pastoral presence. In short, the conflict of interest concern is never resolved.

Rancher-Pontiff

The Rancher-Pontiff (R-P) is usually a charismatic type, skilled in oral persuasion and enjoying a mass following of adherents. The R-P typically divorces himself or herself from denominational or connectional ties. Such alliances are seen as politically disadvantageous, vision restricting, and strategically unnecessary. Ostensibly, heralding the gospel message is the singular duty of R-Ps. R-Ps are more inclined to outsource the relational and communal care congregational ministry obligations to a competent ministry staff of associates she or he puts in place. The R-P's ministry staff—so-called armor bearers—those deemed part of the pastor or bishop's inner circle, have the critical function of protecting his or her life physically but also ensuring that the privacy and desired liberties of the pastor are not encroached upon.

The Rancher-Pontiff's preaching is intensely pragmatic and is oftentimes self-serving; preaching tends to flow out of the preacher's brand. R-Ps are loyal to their methods and faithful to their signature preaching style that people have come to cherish or celebrate. According to R-Ps, preaching that works is evocative and spiritually uplifting. Whether their sermons are entertainment oriented or intensely stern, R-Ps perceive preaching as an event to be experienced. R-Ps are usually gifted storytellers who preach in narrative, didactic, and topical sermon modes.

The strength of the Rancher-Pontiff type resides in his or her ability to draw people of all socioeconomic, racial/ethnic, and generational standing to the worship service. R-Ps take pride in their congregation's capacities to ensure that congregational care resources and cutting-edge technologies are in place and that a comfortable worship environment is provided to attendees. The R-P's preaching and influence is potentially hazardous to the church and community because, beyond their inner circle, their feedback loop tends to be imperceptible. Many R-Ps fall victim to the cult of personality. Finally, as the label *Rancher-Pontiff* suggests, this type enjoys pope-like veneration, and as church leaders, as Samuel J. Gilbert Sr. put it crudely, they do more to corral the sheep than to shepherd them.

Mystic-Spiritualist

The Mystic-Spiritualist (M-S) may be variously defined. But, for our purposes, a M-S is one whose practical ministry concern centers on spiritual encounter. The M-S may see his or her preaching as a vehicle for calling believers into silent prayer. Some M-Ss, who are devoted to the monastic and ascetic life, may believe that the purpose of preaching is to draw that preacher and congregation from worldly concerns. By contrast, other M-Ss may hold the opinion that spiritual encounter must be accompanied by or manifested in speaking in tongues, healing, or some other professed experience of direct apprehension of the Divine by immediate intuition. Almost all M-Ss display confidence in their own power to interpret and communicate God's mysterious intentions in the context of a believing or doubting community.

The Mystic-Spiritualist remains attuned to the existential situation, using gifts of discernment and spiritual meditation. Depending on the setting or what occasioned the M-S's sermons, the sermon may take on any number of forms that are by nature meditational, contemplative, conversational, or exhortative.

The strength of the Mystic-Spiritualist is that in his or her preaching one finds a strong belief that encounter with God often defies rational thought. Another important strength is that preaching is viewed as a form of prayer as well as its fruit. The danger of M-S preaching is that it is prone to promote self-pride; the preacher may view himself or herself as one having secret knowledge to which others are not privy. Finally, because the M-S's inclination or focus is on personal experience there is invariably no tangible apparatus or means for interpreting and naming the spiritual experience experienced.

Social Poet–Technophile

The Social Poet–Technophile (SP-T) pairs social and cultural criticism with his or her Christian faith commitments. SP-Ts are typically innovative. These preachers are generally sought after to take on some parachurch ministry role or perhaps head up a congregation's contemporary worship service alternative to the traditional worship service. SP-Ts incorporate popular music and other cutting-edge technology to perform ministry tasks.

A Social Poet–Technophile's preaching, in general, places strong emphasis on textual relevance and the gospel message's application for contemporary life. SP-T sermons may be inspired by a popular song or movie, a social or political event, or a simple turn of phrase. As the label suggests, technological innovation is deemed friend and never foe to be feared. The use of Blackberries, PDAs, laptops, PowerPoint, podcasts, and blogs to transmit the gospel message is generally preferred by SP-Ts over traditional sermon delivery methods and techniques. SP-Ts understand the power of and increasing demands for visual communication in the primarily oral-aural worship environment. While topical or verse-by-verse expository preaching is the primary approach, a skilled SP-T might transform a pulpit into a spoken-word or poetry slam event.

The strength of the Social Poet–Technophile is that he or she clearly recognizes that since culture is ever evolving and the Christian church must respond to social changes, traditional methods must constantly be scrutinized to assess whether or not they are in need of revision, update, or rejection. Of all the persona types, SP-Ts are the most likely to accommodate to culture uncritically, and thus their preaching might easily be ensnared by the spiritual and theological relativism of secular society.

• • •

When preachers become self-critical and aware of the needs and expectations of their congregations or specialized ministry they better understand what is at stake when they stand to proclaim what "thus saith the Lord." Preachers come in all stripes but carry the same obligation to preach the gospel of love and grace to a dying world. Preaching transforms lives. So, whatever persona(s) defines the preacher's functional identity, he or she must become more in touch with and devoted to what makes his or her voice authentic—Jesus' vision. From this vision the preacher discovers self. Self-discovery is the fruit of a faithful preaching life. The clearer the preacher is about where he or she ought to stand in light of the work assigned to his or her hands, the more profitable that preacher will be to the community that first nurtured his or her faith. When preachers are self-aware about how their social identities communicate to others what God is like, then a higher standard for ministry accountability should be evidenced in our culture. When the masks come down preachers will have to atone for much, but throughout these atonement proceedings African American churches will rise above mediocrity and will start taking ownership of the community revitalization process. When the preacher comes to herself or himself, that preacher goes in search of the home where she or he first lost her or his voice.

Where Do We Go from Here?

If God's human speech in the mouth of the preacher in African America today will hope to have cultural resonance and the capacity to stem the tide of death of the village and supply hope to persons who desperately need social justice, spiritual care, and the community's wisdom, it will need to be homiletical speech that dares to be guided by Jesus' norm-setting inaugural vision for Christian proclamation in Luke 4:16-21. *African American preaching guided in this way is lavishly faithful to its authentic character and charge to the church and the public. It is preaching that speaks justice and hope, intercedes for others sacramentally, and gathers up the community's treasures; its impulse is unashamedly trivocal—prophetic, priestly, and sagely.*

Let me retrace my steps. In chapters 1 through 3, I focused on the state of African American preaching and why it is more threatened than ever imagined. I have argued for African American preachers to reconsider how the prophetic, priestly, and sagely dynamics of preaching enable for them a constructive way for rethinking the preaching ministry in a more well-rounded fashion. Because preaching's purpose is to convey an outlook of the divine plan in the context of community, I have also made the bold claim that the single most important voice to stave off the death of African American churches and communities is that of the preacher. Furthermore, I have sought to describe the nature and function of African American preaching reconsidered trivocally through the prophetic, priestly, and sagely dimensions of the preaching ministry. And in doing this, I have defined this discourse as a *ministry of Christian proclamation communicating God's goodwill toward humankind; a hope-filled discourse about God's expectation of God's creation; a particular expression of spoken Word that finds resources internal to Black life in the North American context.* Then, in chapters 4 and 5 I have offered practical hints and a sermon planning guide for preparing the trivocal sermon, as well as examples of trivocalism in the preaching of representative African American clerics. Finally, having constructed a metaphoric typology of the various self-identities that contemporary Black preachers seem to live out, I have sought in this chapter to provide readers a window into the social world of the Black preacher—that most unique religious personality born out of Black lived experience in North America.

The African American community's dire need for restoration should compel the preacher to function differently—to find a common vision for preaching framed by an open sharing of homiletical perspectives, which is to critique, draw upon, or leverage the resources with which one preacher may fund another. For opposite Jesus' norm-setting declaration of the principal requirements of Christian proclamation recorded in Luke 4 are African American communities staving off their death. What does it mean to proclaim Christ effectively in a disorienting, hypercapitalist, individualistic society? It can only mean naming the crises of the village, thinking through ideological and theological differences, and finding constructive ways to preach three-dimensionally to address the concerns of the village. African American preaching is catalytic and profitable in a violent and fragmented world only when the voices of prophet, priest, and sage, in spoken word, become hopeful proclamation about life in the face of communal death.

A recovered voice in our times speaks life and at the same time answers the command to be silent so that God can be heard among the cacophony of sounds in our information-saturated digital era. In our postmodern culture, even the most faithful preacher will have to own a sad and perplexing truth: there will forever be persons who are resistant and indifferent to the gospel message and to the person who delivers it in the context of lived humanity. Whether one's preaching is faithful to the biblical witness and performed with utmost care, for many, preaching will always be foolish chatter about a story that only a fool could believe—that is, the story of Jesus Christ crucified, buried, risen, and returning to claim his church. Despite this, I have one final confession and hope for African American churches and communities: I believe that every God-summoned, sincere, and faithful preacher of the gospel has the capacity to remake the world as we now know it, and that no preacher will lack something of value to give to the world if God's human speech settles and shapes that preacher's voice. An African American preaching ministry that profits the world is the ministry of both spoken Word and practiced Word. Finally, let me say this: preaching is a gift from God; a gift that "the world didn't give and the world can't take away," as the senior saints would say. The gift of preaching, as James Earl Massey so eloquently put it, is a "burdensome joy." A "burdensome joy" indeed, but for the faithful preacher the gift bestows an invaluable privilege—self-discovery. Let the church say, Amen!

Appendix

A Pocket Map for Four Tasks of Sermon Preparation

Task 1: Exploration

- What drives the preacher to preparation?
  - —Relevant concern or felt need
  - —Exigency or problem to be resolved
  - —Special occasion

- Who's driving and in what direction?
  - —Biblical text →→→→ Rhetorical situation
  - —Rhetorical situation →→→→ Biblical text
  - —Special occasion →→→→ Biblical text or topic-theme

- Assess the rhetorical situation
  - —Will I address a public issue or ecclesial concern?
  - —What is the injustice? Obstacle to be confronted?
  - —What are the facts about the situation?

- Consult the Scriptures
  - —Select text and paraphrase it
  - —What details stand out?

Task 2: Clarification

- Unmask the interpreter
  - —What am I bringing with me?
  - —How am I feeling?

- Exegete biblical text through cultural window
  - Name it
    - What am I lamenting? What can be hoped for? Where is God?
    - Can anything be celebrated? Is there a just pathway or hopeful vision in view?
  - Claim it
    - Listen to the text. What am I hearing?
    - Road test exegesis against trivocal paradigm—prophetic, priestly, and sagely
  - Shape it
    - Bring text and situation into sharp focus
    - Map out two claims; take one on the road

Task 3: Internalization

- Pair exegesis with imagination
  - What am I seeing?
  - What will I say about what I see?

- Determine the movement the sermon will travel
  - Highway (narrative)
  - Point A to point B to point C (traditional)
  - Back and forth (Proctor—dialectical)

- Map it out
- Compose it

Task 4: Proclamation

- Give the vision voice
  - Make it seen; get it said

- Pulpit presentation
  - Speak to shape consciousness; take appropriate risks
  - Find the right pitch; establish a rhythm
  - Offer hopeful symbols; watch for listener cues
  - Value the moment

Annotated Bibliography

Homiletic theory is an integration of theology and method in Christian preaching. The homiletic-theory literature on African American preaching, particularly in the last four decades, has unfolded in three moderately distinct, but interrelated, conceptual orientations:

1. rhetorical-poetical
2. biblical-hermeneutical
3. practical-pastoral theological

Devoted primarily to oral creativity and performance in preaching, the *rhetorical-poetical school* has placed strong emphasis on how the Word becomes an event experienced through the Spirit's power in the speech-act. The personality of the preacher, style of delivery, use of illustrations, and attention to sermon form tend to be the reflective academic focus.

Biblical-hermeneutical school theorists tend to channel in two streams. A few theorists have come into the field with dual disciplinary proficiency, for example, pairing biblical studies with homiletics. They ask how the exegetical process is central to developing sermon content. Others reflect primarily on how Scripture and Christian tradition are used within liturgical contexts.

Finally, the *practical-pastoral theology school's* focus, generally an interdisciplinary one, asks the questions about why theological beliefs, practices, and guiding norms are so central to preaching. The following selected bibliography lists key books for each conceptual orientation.

Rhetorical-Poetical

Crawford, Evans E., Jr. *The Hum: Call and Response in African American Preaching.* Nashville: Abingdon, 1995.

This book focuses on the indigenous oral/aural practice of "call-and-response." Crawford maintains that the oral traditions of "folk art" preaching take seriously the connective dynamics among preacher, sermon, and community.

Davis, Gerald L. *I Got the Word in Me and I Can Sing It, You Know: A Study of the Performed African American Sermon*. Philadelphia: University of Pennsylvania Press, 1985.
This is an important study of the narrative organizational structure of the performed sermon. Davis argues that African American preachers generally can be considered "fundamentalist" because of the manner in which they structure sermons in performance.

Fry Brown, Teresa L. *Delivering the Sermon: Voice, Body, and Animation in Proclamation*. Elements of Preaching. Minneapolis: Fortress Press, 2008.
This concise volume on speech performance in homiletics is an important resource for both novice and experienced preachers about how to communicate the gospel more effectively using voice, body, and animation. Her chapters on vocal and sound production are particularly helpful.

———. *Weary Throats and New Songs: Black Women Proclaiming God's Word*. Nashville: Abingdon, 2003.
Fry Brown's book assesses the distinctive nature of Black women's proclamation. This work provides religious and social critique of the status quo, namely, the exclusion of women from exercising their preaching gifts, and it offers testimonials about how women have told their stories about God and why women must preach in spite of cultural and social resistance.

Lischer, Richard. *The Preacher King: Martin Luther King Jr. and the Word That Moved America*. New York: Oxford University Press, 1995.
This book is clearly the finest homiletical analysis of King's preaching to date. Drawing on a wide compilation of primary source materials (e.g., sermon and speech manuscripts, recordings and interviews and papers), Lischer charts the development of King's oratorical genius from his preacher's kid upbringing to becoming America's most heroic voice of social conscience.

Massey, James Earl. *Designing the Sermon: Order and Movement in Preaching.* Nashville: Abingdon, 1980.

Massey discusses why sermon design is vital for preaching to have a clear path toward its goal to connect the hearer with the grace of God. This book provides the preacher useful "how-to" tools for preaching narrative/story, textual/expository, doctrine/topical, and funeral sermons.

McClain, William B. *Come Sunday: The Liturgy of Zion.* Nashville: Abingdon, 1990.

This companion to the *Songs of Zion* hymnbook examines the breadth and depth of Sunday worship in traditional African American church practice. McClain's most important insights about preaching come in his refusal to divorce Black preaching from its congregational habitat and Black theology commitments.

Mitchell, Henry H. *Black Preaching: The Recovery of a Powerful Art.* Rev. ed. Nashville: Abingdon, 1990.

Mitchell's book is an outgrowth of two separate works, *Black Preaching* (1970), and *The Recovery of Preaching* (1977), based on his 1974 Lyman Beecher Lectures at Yale Divinity School. This landmark text in Black homiletics explores the unique role of preaching in African American culture. This book's primary focus is on the performative-aesthetical dimension of Black preaching as oral folk art.

———. *Celebration and Experience in Preaching.* Nashville: Abingdon, 1990.

This three-part apologetic more clearly situates Mitchell's voice within the New Homiletic school. He argues for "holistic preaching"— a reclaiming of "heart religion" in preaching—and thus focuses on the event and experience of preaching as encounter with the Holy Spirit. Moving away from rationalistic preaching methods, this work stresses the importance of using emotive/intuitive preaching essentials for preaching sermons that celebrate the good news.

Proctor, Samuel D. *The Certain Sound of the Trumpet*. Valley Forge: Judson, 1994.

Proctor's homiletic text is informed by George W. F. Hegel's pattern of "thesis, antithesis, synthesis" problem-solving approach. His sermon-crafting method owes much to the Puritan plain style, which is given to propositional statements and an explication/application sermon form, regardless of the form of the text.

Thomas, Frank A. *They Like to Never Quit Praisin' God: The Role of Celebration in Preaching*. Cleveland: United Church Press, 1997.

Extending Mitchell's theory of celebration, Thomas draws in the work of systems theorists Murray Bowen and Edwin H. Friedman. He makes the case that the notion of "celebration" in preaching is "the natural response" to the gospel.

Biblical-Hermeneutical

Braxton, Brad R. *Preaching Paul*. Nashville: Abingdon, 2004.

Braxton gives the reader a fresh look at the apostle Paul's profile as missionary itinerant preacher. He explores Paul's correspondences to the churches he established in the Greco-Roman world and names them preachable documents. He closely reads the biblical text for homiletical, biblical, and theological clues that may provide useful and constructive ways to share Paul's gospel message in postmodern contexts today.

Forbes, James A., Jr. *The Holy Spirit and Preaching*. Nashville: Abingdon, 1989.

The first line of Forbes's book simply states: "The person who preaches the gospel makes a statement about the Holy Spirit just by entering the pulpit." This book, based on his 1986 Lyman Beecher Lectures at Yale, attempts to bring into focus the role of the Holy Spirit's anointing on the preachers and the preacher's message. This work addresses how spiritual formation should cohere to the preacher's sermon preparation.

Harris, James H. *Preaching Liberation*. Fortress Resources for Preaching. Minneapolis: Fortress Press, 1995.

Harris proposes a biblically based dialectical method for preaching drawing on liberation theology themes. He places special emphasis on God's activity in leading African American people from oppression to liberation. This homiletic is mainly centered on the "what," not the "how," of preaching.

LaRue, Cleophus J., Jr. *The Heart of Black Preaching*. Louisville: Westminster John Knox, 2000.

Drawing on David Kelsey's theological framework, LaRue searches for a hermeneutic that will serve as a "master lens" or template for analyzing the distinctiveness of Black preaching.

Smith, Kelly Miller. *Social Crisis Preaching*. Macon, Ga.: Mercer University Press, 1984.

Smith's book is a compilation of lectures delivered at Yale's 1984 Lyman Beecher Lectures. Beyond a historical and social analysis of Black Christian practices, Smith calls African American churches and Black ministers to be forefront responders to the adverse circumstance and social evils plaguing the health of African American communities. This work focuses on the message of the social gospel, perspectives on race, sermon structure, and the person of the preacher in community.

Smith, Robert, Jr. *Doctrine That Dances: Bringing Doctrinal Preaching and Teaching to Life*. Nashville: B&H, 2008.

Although the practice of preaching and teaching Christian doctrine is centuries old, in this pastoral homiletic, Smith maintains that doctrine will preach, must preach, and must dance rhetorically and poetically if preaching today is to matter and have positive and lasting effect.

Stewart, Warren H., Sr. *Interpreting God's Word in Black Preaching*. Valley Forge: Judson, 1984.

This book is written for preachers and pastors. It attempts to address the relationship between preaching and biblical interpretation (hermeneutics). Stewart supplies a series of sermon excerpts from prominent

African American preachers and offers some prescriptive guiding principles for the preacher's reflection.

Taylor, Gardner C. *How Shall They Preach?* Elgin, Ill.: Progressive Baptist Publishing, 1977.

This volume is derived from Taylor's 1975–76 Lyman Beecher lectures and Lenten sermons he delivered at the historic Concord Baptist Church of Christ in Brooklyn, New York. Taylor not only reminds the preacher about the significance of answering the call to preach but also advises preachers to be humble, introspective, and honest in their preaching, always reminded of their own fragilities.

Practical-Pastoral Theological

Andrews, Dale C. *Practical Theology for Black Churches: Bridging Black Theology and African American Folk Religion.* Louisville: Westminster John Knox, 2002.

This homiletic interprets the estrangement of Black theology from early and contemporary modes of African American folk religion. His ecclesiological analysis of preaching and pastoral care offers invaluable insight.

Bond, L. Susan. *Contemporary African American Preaching: Diversity in Theory and Style.* St. Louis: Chalice, 2003.

Bond surveys the methods of well-known African American homiletical theorists, identifying their similarities and differences through a defined set of eight analytical categories: (1) assumptions about the nature of the gospel; (2) the purpose of preaching; (3) the relationship between preaching and Scripture; (4) the relationship between the Testaments; (5) the nature and purpose of faith communities; (6) the relationship between preaching and liturgy; (7) the relationship of preaching to language theories; and (8) the relationship to other contemporary theological issues.

Brooks, Gennifer. *Good News Preaching: Offering the Gospel in Every Sermon.* Cleveland: Pilgrim, 2009.

This homiletic offers seminarians and working preachers practical strategies for biblical preaching, specifically, how to keep the good news of the gospel of Jesus Christ at the center of the sermon. Brooks believes that good news preaching requires good "homiletical exegesis"—remaining attentive to the gospel preached, the biblical text or topic under consideration, and the manifold needs of an awaiting congregation.

McMickle, Marvin E. *Where Have All the Prophets Gone? Reclaiming Prophetic Preaching in America*. Cleveland: Pilgrim, 2006.
McMickle helpfully points the preacher to take seriously the function and need for prophetic preaching in American society today. He argues that the prophetic biblical literature and having an ear to culture can inspire in pastors tremendous creativity and empower them to address the negative consequences of prosperity preaching and political agendas that have silenced prophetic consciousness in America's pulpits.

Moyd, Olin P. *The Sacred Art: Preaching and Theology in the African American Tradition*. Valley Forge: Judson, 1995.
Moyd's work is developed around two suppositions: (1) African American preaching has historically and is contemporarily the primary vehicle for communicating religious truths and values to the masses of people. (2) Despite diverse African American preaching styles, the basic content of African American preaching, argues Moyd, is practical theology.

Powery, Luke A. *Spirit Speech: Lament and Celebration in Preaching*. Nashville: Abingdon, 2009.
Powery expands the homiletical conversation with his focus on the pneumatological character of African American preaching. Particularly insightful is his claim that our ground of knowing about the manifestation of the Spirit in preaching is found in communal spaces where individual grace finds embrace, ecclesial unity is fostered, and fellowship is encouraged.

Notes

INTRODUCTION

1. Manuel Lee Scott, *From a Black Brother* (Nashville: Broadman, 1971), 88–89.
2. Samuel D. Proctor, *The Certain Sound of the Trumpet* (Valley Forge: Judson, 1994), 11.
3. Gerben Heitink, *Practical Theology: History, Theory, Action Domains,* trans. Reinder Bruinsma (Grand Rapids: Eerdmans, 1999), 120, 130–31.
4. For our purposes, I use the term *African American village* interchangeably with the terms *African America* and *African American churches and communities.* Robert Michael Franklin describes the "village" as the local neighborhoods and communities with predominantly Black populations in the United States. See Robert M. Franklin's *Crisis in the Village: Restoring Hope in African American Communities* (Minneapolis: Fortress Press, 2007), 3.
5. See Brian Blount's book *Cultural Interpretation: Reorienting New Testament Criticism* (Minneapolis: Fortress Press, 1995), 8.
6. Ibid., 23.
7. I am cognizant of the obvious heterogeneity within Black religious life in America. However, there persists a historically constructed African American community in the United States—a critical mass of people of African descent, especially in heavily populated urban areas—whose shared history, cultural memory, and distinctive sociocultural interests are self-evident. Readers will note that the use of the terms *Black* and *African American* and *African American preaching* and *Black preaching* are descriptive labels used interchangeably in this book. The interchangeable use of these terms is standard parlance today in Black studies, African American studies, and increasingly in Black homiletics.

Also, my decision to capitalize the term *Black* is in recognition of the fact that recent scholarship is moving away from the term *black* in lowercase, which primarily suggests an ontological description of identity formation solely based on race. I do not alter the lowercase term *black* when used in direct quotes, however. The capitalization of the term *Black* and not *white* is a way to signal "a rhetorical disruption of domination and white supremacy" and to honor, in a broader fashion, the particular historical and cultural legacy of people of African descent in this country. Frequently used as an alternate expression to the term *African American*, my decision to capitalize the term *Black* also comes from respect for the politics of its fluid and intergenerational usage in the vernacular of persons in communities of African descent. Cf. Ronald Walters and Robert C. Smith's *African American Leadership*

(New York: SUNY Press, 1999), 21; Nancy Lynn Westfield, ed. *Being Black, Teaching Black* (Nashville: Abingdon, 2008), xvi–ii.

8. Walter Brueggemann, "The Prophetic Word of God in History," in *Texts That Linger, Words That Explode: Listening to Prophetic Voices*, ed. Patrick D. Miller (Minneapolis: Fortress Press, 2000), 39–41.

9. Evans E. Crawford. *The Hum: Call and Response in African American Preaching* (Nashville: Abingdon, 1995), 84.

10. Lenora Tubbs Tisdale, *Preaching as Local Theology and Folk Art*, Fortress Resources for Preaching (Minneapolis: Fortress Press, 1997), 53.

11. This schema follows the logic of John Calvin's description of Jesus Christ's threefold office—*prophet, priest,* and *king*—which, according to Calvin, indicates Christ's nature and purpose as Incarnate Word. Cf. *Calvin: Institutes of the Christian Religion I* in Library of Christian Classics, vol. 20, ed. John T. McNeil, trans. Ford Lewis Battles (Philadelphia: Westminster, 1960), 494–503. Instead of the kingly or eldering designation, I use the term *sage* to focus on wisdom's principal role in preaching.

12. See Stephen Farris's discussion in his book *Preaching That Matters* (Louisville: Westminster John Knox, 1998) on specific criteria for preaching "good news" and "bad news" sermons. Farris argues that when a sermon is primarily "bad news" it must pass four tests: (1) the biblical text on which the sermon is based must be primarily bad news; (2) there must be some analogical connection between the people to whom we are preaching and the first recipients of the bad news; (3) we must include ourselves in the message of God's judgment directed toward others; and (4) in the end, words of bad news must be accompanied by words of God's grace and mercy (100).

13. Richard Osmer, *Practical Theology: An Introduction* (Louisville: Westminster John Knox, 2008), 17.

14. Cf. ibid, 11.

CHAPTER I

1. From a Thurman meditation. Audiotape collection, Thurman Listening Room at the Lawrence Neale Jones Library, Howard University School of Divinity.

2. Homiletics, derived from the Greek word *homilia* (often considered synonymous with the Latin word *sermo* or *sermon*) signifies conversation, mutual talk, and thus a familiar discourse. With the influence of rhetoric and the spread of Christianity the homily or sermon became a more formal and extended form of discourse. Moreover, given the inherent interdisciplinary nature of the living practice of preaching, where theology, science, art, and other foci converge, analogous to academic disciplines such as mathematics and physics, the term *homiletics* denotes an academic science or study of the theology and art of preaching. Cf. John Broadus, A *Treatise on the Preparation and Delivery of Sermons* (New York: George H. Doran, 1926 [1870]), 15–16.

3. Some examples are works authored by Henry H. Mitchell, Frank A.Thomas, Teresa Fry-Brown, Dale P. Andrews, Cleophus J. LaRue, and James H. Harris.

4. See Craig Dykstra, "Reconceiving Practice," in *Shifting Boundaries: Contextual Approaches to the Structure of Theological Education*, ed. Barbara G. Wheeler and Edward Farley (Louisville: Westminster John Knox, 1991), 88.

5. Cf. Paulo Freire's definition of cultural invasion in *Pedagogy of the Oppressed*, trans. Myra Bergman Ramos (New York: Continuum, 1970), 150.

6. James Weldon Johnson, *God's Trombones: Seven Negro Sermons in Verse* (New York: Penguin, 1927), 2.

7. Richard F. Ward, *Speaking from the Heart: Preaching with Passion* (Nashville: Abingdon, 1992), 59.

8. Stephen Bevans, *Models of Contextual Theology* (Maryknoll, N.Y.: Orbis, 1992), 1.

9. Dale P. Andrews's *Practical Theology for Black Churches: Bridging Black Theology and African American Folk Religion* (Louisville: Westminster John Knox, 2002); Susan Bond's *Contemporary African American Preaching: Diversity in Theory and Style* (St. Louis: Chalice, 2003); and, more recently, Luke Powery's *Spirit Speech: Lament and Celebration* (Nashville: Abingdon, 2009) are important exceptions.

10. Henry H. Mitchell, *Celebration and Experience in Preaching* (Nashville: Abingdon, 1990), 25.

11. Ibid., 23–24.

12. Ibid., 25.

13. Ibid., 32–34.

14. This new paradigm envisioned the sermon as "event," as distinguished from the "Old Homiletic," which saw the sermon as a product emerging out of a mechanistic molding. The theology ground of the New Homiletic is the New Hermeneutic, a post-Bultmannian existential interpretation derived from the hermeneutics of the later thought of Martin Heidegger.

15. David James Randolph, *The Renewal of Preaching* (Philadelphia: Fortress Press, 1969), 13.

16. For further elaboration, see chapter 5 in Mitchell's book *Black Preaching: The Recovery of a Powerful Art* (Nashville: Abingdon, 1990).

17. Ibid., 78.

18. Cleophus J. LaRue Jr., *The Heart of Black Preaching* (Louisville: Westminster John Knox, 2000), 13.

19. Ibid., 68, 126–27. See also Cleophus J. LaRue, "What Makes Black Preaching Distinctive?: An Investigation Based on Selected African American Sermons from 1865–1915 in Relation to the Hermeneutical Discussion of David Kelsey" (Ph.D. diss., Princeton, 1995), 6–22.

20. LaRue, *The Heart of Black Preaching*, 20.

21. Ibid.

22. Ray, "E-Racing While Black," in Nancy Lynn Westfield, ed., *Being Black, Teaching Black* (Nashville: Abingdon, 2008), 52.

23. See Jonathan L. Walton's sociological analysis of the personality-driven religious phenomenon of contemporary charismatic Black religious broadcasters such as T. D. Jakes, Eddie Long Jr., and Creflo Dollar, who have enjoyed mass followings. *Watch This: The Ethics and Aesthetics of Black Televangelism* (New York: New York University Press, 2008).

24. Ward, *Speaking from the Heart*, 66.

25. Cleophus J. LaRue, "African American Preaching and the Bible," in *True to Our Native Land: An African American New Testament Commentary*, ed. Brian Blount et al. (Minneapolis: Fortress Press, 2007), 65.

26. Martin Luther King Jr., "Shattered Dreams," in *Strength to Love* (Philadelphia: Fortress Press, 1981), 91.

27. Robert M. Franklin, *Crisis in the Village: Restoring Hope in African American Communities* (Minneapolis: Fortress Press, 2007), 3.

28. Ibid., 13.

29. Ibid., 112. See Milmon Harrison's book *Righteous Riches: The Word of Faith Movement in Contemporary African American Religion* (New York: Oxford University Press, 2005) for a careful survey of the broad landscape of the movement in the context of American religion. Harrison argues that the Word of Faith or "prosperity message" is essentially a mixture of evangelicalism, neo-Pentecostalism, and, most important, New Thought metaphysics. Accordingly, three characteristics from this diverse ancestry form its core doctrine: (1) the principle of knowing who you are in Christ, (2) the practice of positive confession (positive thinking), and (3) a worldview centered on material prosperity and physical health as divine right of every Christian. For this reason poverty is seen as a curse in the Word of Faith doctrine.

CHAPTER 2

1. W. E. B. Du Bois, *The Souls of Black Folk* (Canada: General Pub. Co., 1994 [1903]), 119.

2. James Farmer, *Lay Bare Thy Heart: An Autobiography of the Civil Rights Movement* (New York: Arbor House, 1985), 33.

3. It will become apparent that my tracing ends after the civil rights period of the 1950s and '60s. My decision not to venerate contemporary African American clergy and their contributions to the development and advancement of Black preaching is a conscious one. I am convinced that Martin Luther King Jr.'s death, in many ways, activated a preaching nadir in African American contexts.

4. Gayraud Wilmore, *Black Religion and Black Radicalism: An Interpretation of the Religious History of African Americans*, 3d ed. (Maryknoll, N.Y.: Orbis, 1998), 24–25, 36.

5. Quoted from Janheinz Jahn's *Muntu: African Culture and the Western World* (New York: Grove, 1990), in Adisa A. Alkebulan's essay, "The Spiritual Essence of African American Rhetoric," in *Understanding African American Rhetoric: Classical Origins to Contemporary Innovations*, ed. Ronald L. Jackson II and Elaine B. Richardson (New York: Routledge, 2003), 32.

6. John S. McClure, *Preaching Words: 144 Key Terms in Homiletics* (Louisville: Westminster John Knox, 2007), 96.

7. Molefi K. Asante, *The Afrocentric Idea*, rev. and exp. ed. (Philadelphia: Temple University Press, 1998), 30.

8. Alkebulan, "The Spiritual Essence of African American Rhetoric," 29, citing Jahn.

9. Eugene D. Genovese, *Roll, Jordan, Roll: The World the Slaves Made* (New York: Vintage, 1976), 255.

10. Ibid., 255–60.

11. Ibid., 38.

12. Dolan Hubbard, *The Sermon and the African American Literary Imagination* (Columbia: University of Missouri Press, 1994), 2.

13. Eddie Glaude, *Exodus! Religion, Race, and Nation in Early Nineteenth-Century Black America* (Chicago: University of Chicago Press, 2000), 3–4.

14. Hubbard, *The Sermon and the African American Literary Imagination*, 2.

15. Genovese, *Roll, Jordan, Roll*, 263, 272.

16. James Weldon Johnson, *God's Trombones: Seven Negro Sermons in Verse* (New York: Penguin, 1927), 3.

17. Genovese, *Roll, Jordan, Roll*, 269. See Evans E. Crawford's *The Hum: Call and Response in African American Preaching* (Nashville: Abingdon, 1995) for a more extensive analysis of the nature and sociocultural function of this indigenous tradition.

18. Youtha C. Hardman-Cromwell, "'Freedom From' in Negro Preaching of the Nineteenth Century," *American Transcendental Quarterly* 14, no. 2 (December 2000): 282.

19. William E. Hatcher, *John Jasper: The Unmatched Negro Philosopher and Preacher* (New York: Revell, 1908), 10. The invisible church refers to slave religion prior to the Civil War.

20. Cleophus J. LaRue Jr., *The Heart of Black Preaching* (Louisville: Westminster John Knox, 2000), 68, 126–27.

21. Licensed as a local preacher by white Baptists, Virginia-born Brooke County, Georgia, slave preacher George Liele preached widely, both to his own congregation of Black parishioners and on different plantations in the late eighteenth century. Liele later journeyed to Kingston, Jamaica, in 1782. Two years later he established the first Baptist church on the island, which grew to 350 parishioners. Coming to conversion after hearing Liele's preaching on "being born again" in Savannah, nearly a year after Liele's departure from Savannah's Silver Bluff church, Andrew Bryan was licensed and ordained, becoming the church's pastor in 1788, where he preached to Blacks and a few whites (Cf. John W. Davies, "George Liele and Andrew Bryan: Pioneer Negro Baptist Preachers," in *The Journal of Negro History* 3, no. 2 (April 1918): 119–20, 124. While Black preachers mostly assumed primarily a role of politically passive realism, as Genovese has suggested, prior to the Civil War, astonishingly, over one hundred Black Baptist preachers had become ordained ministers. See also Albert J. Raboteau, *Slave Religion: The "Invisible Institution" in the Antebellum South* (New York: Oxford University Press, 1978), 140; Cleophus J. LaRue Jr., ed., *Power in the Pulpit: How America's Most Effective Black Preachers Prepare Their Sermons* (Louisville: Westminster John Knox, 2002), 3. Cf. Mechal Sobel, *Trabelin' On: The Slave Journey to an Afro-Baptist Faith* (Princeton: Princeton University Press, 1980).

22. Albert J. Raboteau, "Black Christianity in North America," in *Encyclopedia of the American Religious Experience: Studies of Traditions and Movements*, vol. 1, ed. Charles H. Lippy and Peter W. Williams (New York: Charles Scribner's Sons, 1988), 635.

23. Faith Vibert, "Society of the Propagation of the Gospel," *The Journal of Negro History* 18 (1993): 212.

24. Raboteau, "Black Christianity in North America," 636.

25. Genovese, *Roll, Jordan, Roll*, 258.

26. Ibid.

27. Ibid., 256.

28. Ibid., 257.

29. Excerpted from David Walker, "David Walker's Appeal in Four Articles; Together with a Preamble, to the Coloured Citizens of the World, but in Particular and Very Expressly, to those of the United States of America (Boston: Revised and published by David Walker, 3rd ed., 1830)," in *Let Nobody Turn Us Around: Voices of Resistance, Reform, and Renewal, An African American Anthology*, ed. Manning Marable and Leith Mullings (New York: Rowman & Littlefield, 2000), 26.

30. Genovese, *Roll, Jordan, Roll*, 257.

31. Ibid., 272–73.

32. Cf. Albert J. Raboteau, "The Black Experience in American Evangelicalism: The Meaning of Slavery," in *Evangelical Tradition in America*, ed. Leonard Sweet (Macon, Ga.: Mercer University Press, 1984), 181–84.

33. Ibid.

34. Ibid. See Donald G. Mathews, *Religion in the Old South*, ed. Martin F. Marty, Chicago History of American Religion (Chicago: University of Chicago Press, 1977).

35. Raboteau, "Black Christianity in North America," 636.

36. Ibid.

37. Mathews, *Religion in the Old South*, 190.

38. Evidently, Hatch grossly overstates the fact that whites welcomed Blacks as full participants in their communities since that would have implied social equality. His point that there were signs that early white evangelicals were friendly toward freedom is most pertinent here. Nathan O. Hatch, *The Democratization of American Christianity* (New Haven: Yale University Press, 1989), 102–106.

39. Ibid.

40. Raboteau cites quote from Fisk University, *Unwritten History of Slavery: Autobiographical Accounts of Negro Ex-slaves* (Washington, D.C.: NCR Microcard Editions, 1968), 108.

41. Mathews, *Religion in the Old South*, 250.

42. Albert J. Raboteau, *Canaan Land: A Religious History of African Americans* (New York: Oxford University Press, 1999), 23. Cf. Clarence E. Walker, *A Rock in a Weary Land: The African Methodist Episcopal Church During the Civil War and Reconstruction* (Baton Rouge: Louisiana State University Press, 1982), 4.

43. Peter J. Paris, *The Social Teaching of the Black Churches* (Philadelphia: Fortress Press, 1985), 46.

44. Mathews, *Religion in the Old South*, 247. Rayford Logan points to this unconscionable reality (religious hypocrisy of whites) when he declares, "Churches that denied membership to Negroes still preached the Fatherhood of God and the Brotherhood of Man." Cf. Rayford W. Logan, *The Betrayal of the Negro: From Rutherford B. Hayes to Woodrow Wilson* (New York: Collier, 1965), 314.

45. Mathews, *Religion in the Old South*, 250.

46. Ibid., 213.

47. The belief that Jesus will return to earth prior to a period of one thousand years during which he will reign, combined with a system of spirituality that emphasizes waiting on God.

48. Sydney E. Ahlstrom, *A Religious History of the American People* (New Haven: Yale University Press, 1972), 690.

49. See Cain's biographic profile at http://www.blackpast.org/?q=aah/cain-richard-h-1825-1887, accessed June 24, 2010.

50. Benjamin E. Mays and Joseph W. Nicholson, *The Negro's Church* (New York: Institute of Social and Religious Research, 1933).

51. Raboteau, "The Black Experience in American Evangelicalism," 181–97.

52. Wallace Best, *Passionately Human, No Less Divine: Religion and Culture in Black Chicago 1915–1952* (Princeton: Princeton University Press, 2005), 40. Beginning at the first phase of the migration, social theorists were classifying Black migrants into categories of lower, working, middle, and elite classes. Accordingly, Blacks, too, internalized these criteria of social distinction along class lines as a way to avoid class permeation in certain churches. But even before the Civil War those Blacks who held membership in Episcopal churches were of the Black aristocracy.

53. Best, *Passionately Human*, 3, 8.

54. Milton C. Sernett, *Bound for the Promised Land: African American Religion and the Great Migration* (Durham: Duke University Press, 1997), 3.

55. Ibid., 64. Cf. Thomas T. Woofter, *Southern Race Progress: The Wavering Color Line* (Washington, D.C.: Public Affairs, 1957), 59. See Appendix A, Thomas Watson Harvey, interview by Giles R. Wright, April 30, 1976, transcript, New Jersey Multi-Ethnic Oral History Project, Trenton, N.J.

56. Sernett, *Bound for the Promised Land*, 72.

57. Ibid., 73.

58. Ibid. The author illustrates this notion by recounting the influential voice of Henry H. Proctor, pastor of the first Black institutional church in Atlanta. Proctor, he quotes, "gave a series of lectures in which he argued that the antidote to migration fever was not all that mysterious; whites must give Blacks 'a square deal, based on the golden rule.'"

59. Ibid., 74.

60. Ibid., 116.

61. Carol Marks, *Farewell—We're Good and Gone* (Bloomington: Indiana University Press, 1989), 32.

62. Harvey, "New Jersey Multi-Ethnic Oral History Project." S. P. Fullinwider corroborates Harvey's recollection of Walker's notoriety in *The Mind and Mood of Black America: 20th Century Thought* (Homewood, Ill.: Dorsey, 1969). Fullinwider notes that Walker achieved fame in the 1880s, and gained the reputation as the "Black Spurgeon" in a way reminiscent of Booker T. Washington (31). Ironically, by 1901 Walker had been named pastor of two prominent congregations in the North and South, Tabernacle Baptist in Augusta and Mt. Olivet Baptist in New York. Cf. Silas X. Floyd. *The Life of Charles T. Walker* (New York: Negro Universities Press, 1969 [1902]), a biography with sermon extracts published before the migration tide (115–23).

63. Hans A. Baer, *The Black Spiritual Movement: A Religious Response to Racism* (Knoxville: University of Tennessee, 1984), 18. Though a vague term, "Spiritualist" refers to those religious groups that believe in "communication of the spirit," or relaying messages and spirits through mediums. Cf. Allen H. Spear, *Black Chicago: The Making of a Negro Ghetto, 1890–1920* (Chicago: University of Chicago Press, 1967), 177.

64. Baer claims that pastors of these churches are almost always mediums possessing the ability to read people and exhort to them words about their past, present, and future (*The Black Spiritual Movement*, 50–51).

65. Sernett, *Bound for the Promised Land*, 43.

66. Ibid., 53.

67. Ibid., 163.

68. Thurman Garner and Carolyn Calloway-Thomas, "African American Orality: Expanding Rhetoric," in *Understanding African American Rhetoric: Classic Origins to Contemporary Innovations*, ed. Ronald L. Jackson II and Elaine B. Richardson (New York: Routledge, 2003), 46.

69. Marks, *Farewell—We're Good and Gone*, 32.

70. See James M. Washington, "Editor's Introduction: Martin Luther King, Jr., Martyred Prophet for a Global Beloved Community of Justice, Faith, and Hope," in Washington, ed., *A Testament of Hope: The Essential Writings and Speeches of Martin Luther King, Jr.* (New York: HarperCollins, 1986), xii.

71. Raboteau, *Canaan Land*, 113.

72. Du Bois, *The Souls of Black Folk*, 116.

CHAPTER 3

1. Gerbern Heitink, *Practical Theology: History, Theory, Action Domains*, trans. Reinder Bruinsma (Grand Rapids: Eerdmans, 1999), 120, 130–31.

2. Walter Brueggemann, *A Commentary on Jeremiah: Exile and Homecoming* (Grand Rapids: Eerdmans, 1998), 78.

3. Ibid., 12.

4. Jeremiah was the son of Hilkiah, of the priest of Anathoth (likely descendents of Abiathar, a priest in David's court banished for aligning himself with David's rival Adonijah); see Jeremiah 1.

5. Outside the Temple motif, Jeremiah functions as a priest sent by God to declare a word of hope and comfort to God's people taken into Babylonian exile (see 29:11-14).

6. Albert J. Raboteau, "The Black Experience in American Evangelicalism: The Meaning of Slavery," in *Evangelical Tradition in America*, ed. Leonard Sweet (Macon, Ga.: Mercer University Press, 1984), 195–97.

7. Penny Edgell Becker, *Congregations in Conflict: Cultural Models of Local Religious Life* (New York: Cambridge University Press), 13.

8. Harold Dean Trulear, "African American Religious Education," in *Multicultural Religious Education*, ed. Barbara Wilkerson (Birmingham: Religious Education Press, 1997), 120.

9. Marvin McMickle, *Preaching to the Black Middle Class* (Valley Forge: Judson, 1999), 25.

10. Peter J. Paris, *The Social Teaching of the Black Churches* (Philadelphia: Fortress Press, 1985), 11. In all fairness, it is worth mentioning that McMickle's recent work *Where Have All the Prophets Gone?* (Cleveland: Pilgrim, 2006) ably profiles his concern for prophetic preaching.

11. Alyce M. McKenzie, *Preaching Biblical Wisdom in a Self-Help Society* (Nashville: Abingdon, 2002), 35.

12. Alyce M. McKenzie, *Preaching Proverbs: Wisdom for the Pulpit* (Louisville: Westminster John Knox, 1996), xxi.

13. Ibid., 117.

14. See "The Black Church Is Dead," https://www.huffingtonpost.com/eddie-glaude-jr-phd/the-black-church-is-dead_b_473815.html.

15. For a more detailed discussion of these models, see Richard R. Osmer, *Practical Theology: An Introduction* (Grand Rapids: Eerdmans), 164–73.

16. Ibid., 170–73.

17. Ibid., 167.

18. Matthew Lamb, *Solidarity with Victims: Toward a Theology of Social Transformation* (New York: Crossroad, 1982), 1.

19. Ibid., 11.

20. Ibid.

21. James E. Loder, "Normativity and Context in Practical Theology: The Interdisciplinary Issue," in *Practical Theology: International Perspectives*, ed. Friedrich Schweitzer and Johannes A. Van der Ven Beren (Frankfort am Main: Peter Lang, 1999), 359.

22. Ibid., 361–62.

23. Ibid., 363.

24. Dale Andrews, *Practical Theology for Black Churches: Bridging Black Theology and African American Folk Religion* (Louisville: Westminster John Knox, 2002), 7.

25. Ibid., 4.

26. Ibid., 51, 56.

27. Ibid., 34.

28. Ibid., 40–42.

29. Ibid., 42–44.

30. Ibid., 44–45.

31. Ibid., 45–46.

32. Ibid., 86.

33. Ibid., 91.

34. Ibid.

CHAPTER 4

1. Nathan Dell, "A Prince and a Great Man: Eulogy of Miles Jerome Jones," *The African American Pulpit* 8, no. 2 (Spring 2005), 75.

2. Samuel D. Proctor, *The Certain Sound of the Trumpet* (Valley Forge: Judson, 1995), 9.

3. Ibid., 435–37.

4. David Bartlett, "Sermon," in *Concise Encyclopedia of Preaching*, ed. William Willimon and Richard Lischer (Louisville: Westminster John Knox, 1995), 433–35.

5. Henry Ward Beecher, "Personal Elements in Preaching," in *Yale Lectures on Preaching*, vol. 1 (New York: J. B. Ford, 1872), 77.

6. Lloyd Bitzer, "The Rhetorical Situation," in *Philosophy and Rhetoric*, 1, 1–14, reprinted in John Louis Lucaites, Celeste Michelle Condit, Sally Caudill, eds., *Contemporary Rhetorical Theory: A Reader* (New York: Guilford, 1999), 217, 220.

7. Charles G. Adams, "Preaching from the Heart and Mind," in *Power in the Pulpit: How America's Most Effective Preachers Prepare Their Sermons*, ed. Cleophus J. LaRue (Louisville: Westminster John Knox, 2002), 15.

8. See Marvin McMickle's *Shaping the Claim: Moving from Text to Sermon*, Elements of Preaching (Minneapolis: Fortress Press, 2008), 6–7.

9. Lecture by Dr. Sally Brown at Princeton Theological Seminary, 2001.

10. Cf. H. Grady Davis's *Design for Preaching* (Philadelphia: Muhlenberg, 1958).

11. James Earl Massey, *Designing the Sermon: Order and Movement in Preaching* (Nashville: Abingdon, 1980), 20.

12. Henry H. Mitchell, *Celebration and Experience in Preaching* (Nashville: Abingdon, 1990), 29–30.

13. William B. McClain, *Come Sunday: The Liturgy of Zion* (Nashville: Abingdon, 1990), 67–68.

14. Cf. Luke Powery's recent book *Spirit Speech: Lament and Celebration in Preaching* (Nashville: Abingdon, 2009).

15. Thomas G. Long, *The Witness of Preaching*, 2d ed. (Louisville: Westminster John Knox, 2000), 97.

16. Teresa Fry Brown, *Delivering the Sermon: Voice, Body, and Animation in Proclamation*, Elements of Preaching (Minneapolis: Fortress Press, 2008), 8.

17. Gloria H. Albrecht, *The Character of Our Communities: Toward an Ethic of Liberation for the Church* (Nashville: Abingdon, 1995), 37.

18. Allen Dwight Callahan, "The Gospel of John," in *True to Our Native Land: An African American New Testament Commentary*, ed. Brian K. Blount et al. (Minneapolis: Fortress Press, 2007), 199.

19. Howard Thurman, "Pain Has a Ministry," in *Meditations of the Heart* (Boston: Beacon, 1953, 1981), 65.

20. Henri J. Nouwen, *The Wounded Healer: Ministry in Contemporary Society* (New York: Image Books/Doubleday, 1972).

21. Dietrich Bonhoeffer, *The Cost of Discipleship*, rev. exp. ed (New York: Macmillan, 1963 [1937]), 99.

22. M. Scott Peck, *The Road Less Traveled* (New York: Touchstone, 1978), 15.

23. See Sally A. Brown's helpful discussion of these theories of atonement in *Cross Talk: Preaching Redemption Here and Now* (Louisville: Westminster John Knox, 2009).

24. *Common English Bible (CEB): New Testament: A Fresh Translation to Touch the Heart and Mind* (Nashville: Christian Resources, 2010).

25. Samuel D. Proctor and Gardner C. Taylor, with Gary V. Simpson, *We Have This Ministry: The Heart of the Pastor's Vocation* (Valley Forge: Judson, 1996), 136.
26. Ruben A. Alves, *A Theology of Human Hope* (St. Meinrad, Ind.: Abbey, 1974), x.

CHAPTER 5

1. Charles E. Booth, "What Ever Happened to Hermeneutics?," in *The African American Pulpit* 6, no. 4 (Fall 2003): 7–8.
2. Joel C. Gregory, "Measuring a Preacher's Creativity with a Borrowed Ruler," in *Our Sufficiency Is of God: Essays on Preaching in Honor of Gardner C. Taylor*, ed. Timothy George, James Earl Massey, and Robert Smith Jr. (Macon, Ga.: Mercer University Press, 2010), 44.
3. James Melvin Washington has alternatively titled this sermon, "I See the Promised Land." Cf. *A Testimony of Hope: The Essential Writings and Speeches of Martin Luther King, Jr.*, ed. James M. Washington (New York: HarperCollins, 1986), 279–86.
4. Ibid.
5. Ibid., 286.
6. Ibid., 280.
7. Ibid., 281.
8. Ibid.
9. Ibid.
10. Ibid., 282.
11. Prathia Hall, "Between the Wilderness and the Cliff," *The African American Pulpit* 10, no. 9 (Summer 2007): 44–48.
12. Ibid., 46.
13. Ibid., 48.
14. Ibid., 47.
15. Gardner C. Taylor, "Parting Words," in *The Words of Gardner Taylor*, vol. 4: *Special Occasion and Expository Sermons* (Valley Forge: Judson, 2001), 109–13.
16. Ibid., 110–11.
17. Ibid., 112–13.
18. Ibid., 109.
19. Ibid., 112–13.
20. Though Forbes until January 2007 served the 2,400-member Riverside Church—a interdenominational, interracial, and international congregation affiliated with both the American Baptist Churches and the United Church of Christ, built by John D. Rockefeller Jr., and celebrated for its long-standing concern for social justice—he nonetheless preaches widely and remains connected to his African American heritage and religious roots. Forbes is an ordained minister in the American Baptist Churches and the Original United Holy Church of America (a predominantly Black Holiness Pentecostal denomination).
21. James A. Forbes Jr., "No Time for Foolishness!" available at http://rockefeller.uchicago.edu/Sermons/guests/110903sermon.html, accessed July 1, 2010.

22. The Reverend Dr. DeForest B. Soaries Jr. is senior pastor of First Baptist Church of Lincoln Gardens in Somerset, New Jersey. This is a transcription of a sermon audio recorded at FBCLG in 2005. For a number of years he has rallied the congregation around a vision of becoming a "debt-free" church. FBCLG is the featured congregation on CNN's recent documentary "Almighty Debt: A Black in America Special," with Soledad O'brien, airing on October 21, 2010.

23. The Reverend Dr. Jeremiah Wright Jr. is pastor emeritus of the largest congregation of his denomination, the 8,500-member Trinity United Church of Christ (UCC) in Chicago, Illinois. On the occasion of Howard University School of Divinity's Ninetieth Convocation in 2006, he addressed a gathering of UCC African American ministers and members of the Divinity School. I should note that Wright holds the attention-grabbing distinction of being President Barack Obama's pastor prior to and during his tenure as a U.S. senator. Though Wright and Obama's politics are not always necessarily aligned, it is interesting to observe their distinctive attitudes toward language and rhetoric as a means of conveying cultural self-definition within the public sphere. Both Obama (in his tenure as a member of the Senate Foreign Relations committee) and the Reverend Wright were critical of the Bush administration's failures in the war in Iraq along with domestic policy issues. Wright's righteous indignation, however, as illustrated in the sermon delivered in Howard University's Divinity School's Thurman Chapel, is speech not typically heard in the halls of Congress.

24. Jeremiah A. Wright Jr., "Reclaiming Prophetic Ministry: It's Hard Out Here for a Prophet." Sermon preached at the 90th Annual Convocation of Howard University School of Divinity in cooperation with the United Church of Christ African American Ministers' Second Annual Conference, Wednesday, November 1, 2006, in Howard Thurman Chapel.

25. Walter Brueggemann, *The Prophetic Imagination*, rev. ed. (Minneapolis: Fortress Press, 2002), 3–4.

26. Wright, "Reclaiming Prophetic Ministry."

27. J. Alfred Smith Sr. is clearly a sagely voice and presence in the field of homiletics and is renowned for his work as preacher-pastor-practitioner; however, I am highlighting this particular sermon in the prophetic category because it is perhaps the best-written prophetically grounded contemporary sermon that I have read. J. Alfred Smith Sr., "Preaching to the Cities," *The African American Pulpit* 12, no. 2 (Spring 2009): 86–91.

28. Ibid., 87.

29. Ibid., 89.

30. Ibid., 90–91.

31. Ibid., 91.

32. Wayne C. Croft Sr. is senior pastor of the Church of the Redeemer Baptist in Philadelphia, Jeremiah A. Wright Sr. Associate Professor of Homiletics and Liturgics in African American Studies at Lutheran Theological Seminary at Philadelphia. His PhD dissertation is about eschatology and hope in African American preaching.

33. Wayne C. Croft Sr., "A Candidate for the Hall of Faith," *The African American Pulpit* 12, no. 1 (Winter 2008–2009): 44.

34. Noel Jones is senior pastor of City of Refuge Church in Gardenia, California, and founder of Noel Jones Ministries. He is an ordained bishop in the Pentecostal Assemblies of the World.

35. Noel Jones, "Help Me, Holy Ghost," *The African American Pulpit* 10, no. 4 (Fall 2007): 63.

36. Cf. 1 John 4:4; ibid.

37. Ibid.

38. Gennifer B. Brooks is Director of the Styberg Preaching Institute and is associate professor of homiletics at Garrett-Evangelical Theological Seminary in Evanston, Illinois.

39. Gennifer B. Brooks, "A Matter of Choice," *The African American Pulpit* 9, no. 1 (Winter 2005–06): 39.

40. The complete sermon manuscript is published in Braxton's book *Preaching Paul* (Nashville: Abingdon, 2004), 147–55.

41. Ibid., 147.

42. Ibid., 148.

43. Ibid., 151.

44. Ibid., 153.

45. In July 2000, Violet Fisher was consecrated as a bishop in the United Methodist Church.

46. Violet L. Fisher, "Bread for the Journey," *The African American Pulpit* 12, no. 2 (Spring 2009): 40.

47. Ibid.

48. Ibid., 41.

49. Haywood Robinson III serves the People's Community Baptist Church in Silver Spring, Maryland. This excerpt was transcribed from a sermon audio-recorded on January 3, 2010.

50. William D. Watley serves as senior pastor of the historic St. James African Methodist Episcopal Church, in Newark, New Jersey.

51. William D. Watley, "Two Roads to the Same Place," *The African American Pulpit* 4, no. 4 (Fall 2001): 97.

52. *The African American Pulpit* 5, no. 4 (Fall 2002): 4.

53. Samuel J. Gilbert Sr., "How to Handle Conflict in the World," ibid., 17.

54. Ibid., 19.

55. Samuel J. Gilbert II, "A Dedication to the Cause of Christ," ibid., 21–22.

CHAPTER 6

1. Martin Luther King Jr., "I See the Promised Land (3 April 1968)," in *A Testament of Hope: The Essential Writings and Speeches of Martin Luther King, Jr.*, ed. James M. Washington (New York: HarperCollins, 1986), 282.

2. Thomas G. Long, *The Witness of Preaching*, 2d ed. (Louisville: Westminster John Knox, 2005), 18.

3. See H. Beecher Hicks Jr.'s study, *Images of the Black Preacher: The Man Nobody Knows* (Valley Forge: Judson, 1977), where he offers a descriptive analysis of Black preacher profiles from slavery forward.

Index